Finding the Limits

Tales of an average ultra runner

Douglas Lawson

DISCLAIMER

The purpose of this book is to share my journey of how I progressed from walking to school, to running ultra marathons. While I do encourage others to be active and increase their fitness levels, the publishers and I take no responsibility for any injuries, accidents, or mishaps that may occur to individuals who try to copy anything I have done in this book. If you wish to participate in running or any other form of fitness training, I encourage you to seek medical and professional advice first. Adventures are only fun if you can walk away from them and live to tell the tale afterwards.

Email: DouglasLawson70@outlook.com
Facebook: @DouglasLawsonAuthor
Twitter: @DLawson_Author

Dedicated to Claire, Logan, and Owen.
My inspiration.

Contents

Chapter 1

From Humble Beginnings

Running was never a word I enjoyed hearing as a child, the only time I ever really did any running was when I was either fleeing from bullies, or avoiding a beating from my mother for being mischievous. Running was something I wasn't really cut out to do, I was a small child and slow to develop physically, so slow in fact that my childhood nickname was "Diddy", a name used by my friends to describe my small stature. I was also very shy and meek, I lacked confidence in myself, which made me an easy target for bullies.

I grew up in quite a rough area of Coventry, and the secondary school I went to had a bad reputation. A large part of my time in school was dodging punches and hiding from packs of roaming bullies. Little did I know at the time that this was perfect training for a future career in the military. From an early age I became an expert at running from cover to cover, and avoiding the constant onslaught of the enemy.

The only other time I ran in school was in physical education classes, lessons so brutal in their nature, which should they happen today, the school would be investigated for their disregard for human life. We were forced to play rugby in January, on pitches frozen so solid, the mud was as hard as granite and the grass as sharp as glass. By the time the lesson came to an end the rugby pitch would resemble a medieval battle field, cries of agony would drift through the frozen mist, and many of the fallen needed urgent medical attention and blood transfusions.

I never really took to sport in my early teens, football and rugby were a requirement in school, however I never followed any teams or even watched any games, so my enthusiasm for participating in these events was low to zero.

My small physical size and lack of athletic ability was never more obvious though than when it came to track running. Sure there were other children of my age and size in our school year, however I never seemed to be pitted against them when it came to running, I would always be up against the very best runners. One person I always ended up being drawn against was RB, he was of Jamaican decent, a good 2 feet taller than me, muscled, and the perfect definition of athletic performance.

We would do 200 meter sprints, and he would be a good 10 meters in front of me before I'd even taken my first stride, it was like pitting the Wright Brothers plane against a Eurofighter Typhoon. I was always savagely annihilated in these sprints, and my spirit would be crushed. It used to feel like an eternity to get to the finish line, and RB would have arrived a good half a minute before me and be doing stretches there, while I would be staggering across the line, holding my sides and in need of a ventilator.

Apart from the short sharp bolts I did to avoid bullies as a child, speed was never my specialty. I was however good at the long plod. I could go slowly for quite long periods. My parents' house was half a mile away from my school, and I used to go home for school dinners. I had a 1 hour window for lunch break and in that time I would plod home, eat my lunch, then plod back to school. This distance accompanied by my walking in and home, added up to 2 miles a day I was traveling just by going to and from school, I didn't know it at the time but this was building a good foundation for traveling large distances on my legs.

I left school at age 15 and started working in a small engineering factory near Coventry City Centre. These were still early days in my journey to adulthood and I hadn't learned how to drive yet. I was also reluctant to take the bus to my work place as its timetable was sporadic at best, and then when it did turn up, it usually housed junkies or glue sniffers. So I used to walk to work. This was some 4 miles distant, so going into and coming home from work amounted to me amalgamating 8 miles a day in distance.

At age 19 I finally had enough of Coventry and its violent tendencies, I grew tired of seeing people get shot in the local news, and I was sick of walking on eggshells around my neighbourhood. One day while on my lunch break I saw an advert in the paper I was reading - "Join the Army and see the world." It showed images of jungles and deserts, mountains and moorlands, places so exotic and distant from my current existence they could have been on another planet. There were images of off duty soldiers skiing, and laughing on beaches, it looked amazing and sent my heart racing. Yes I knew at the time a career in the military wasn't all sunshine and roses, but as I summed up the pros and cons, I realised there was actually less chance of me getting shot on a battle field than living where I did.

The following day I found myself in the local Army careers office begging to join. I originally applied for the Army Air Corps, however I was told that they were at full capacity and it could be a wait of a year for me to be accepted. I was so desperate to get out of Coventry at that time, I changed my application and applied for the infantry, and Coventry's local regiment – The Royal Regiment of Fusiliers.

During my first interview with a deceivingly friendly Staff Sergeant, I was asked what my fitness levels were like. I instantly brushed the question away replying that they were fantastic, after all I had been walking 8 miles a day for the last few years commuting to work. He then went on to list the fitness tests I would have to pass at the selection centre that I would need to attend - A certain amount of press-ups and sit-ups in a fixed time period, a minimum number of pull-ups, etc.

He then went on to say I needed to pass a run test called the B.F.T (Basic Fitness Test), a 1.5 mile run that had to be completed in under 10minutes 30seconds. To me at the time 10 and half minutes to complete 1.5 miles sounded like a breeze, how wrong I was.

That evening I put on my tracksuit and training shoes, and headed over to the local school which had a 400 meter running track. The start lines had worn off, so I placed a stick in the ground to indicate where I had started, and so I would know when I'd achieved a full lap. I was pumped up and ready to go, and I took off at a moderate pace. Within half a lap I was gasping for breath, and by the time I approached the stick indicating that I had completed 1 lap; a mere quarter of a mile, I was struggling in a big way. I continued on, after another half a lap however I found myself having to walk. As I approached the stick for a second time, I just collapsed on the floor next to it feeling completely deflated and defeated. "How can I be this unfit?" I remember gasping to myself.

That was a big defining moment for me, as I shuffled back to my parents' house, I felt completely dejected. I was sure I could not make the minimum fitness level to join the army. As I lay in bed that night I made a promise to myself that this would not beat me, I would get myself fit if it killed me.

The following morning I woke early and decided rather than walking slowly into work, I would start jogging there. At first this was very tough indeed, I was start-stopping all the way in, and feeling exhausted at the start of the work day, then I would have to repeat the process on the way home. After a mere 2 weeks however things started to improve, my energy levels increased and I could go further each time before I had to walk. Eventually I started timing myself how long it would take me each day to get to work, then try to beat that time the following day, it became a mini obsession.

After 1 month I tested myself on the school running track again, and to my amazement I found I could do 4 laps (1 mile) before I started to struggle some, it was a huge improvement in my fitness level, and in quite a short period of time. My confidence soared, and I had hope again that I may indeed be able to make the fitness requirement.

I received a letter 2 days after this inviting me to attend the army recruitment test weekend at Litchfield Barracks. Excitement pumped through my veins again, and I felt I was ready.

So far I had only focused on the fitness requirements needed for a military career and not the crushing discipline that goes with it, this however became all too evident when I stepped off the train at Litchfield station with 30 other potential recruits, and we were shepherded into the barracks.

We were quickly formed up into 3 lines on a parade ground and subjected to a torrent of abuse, screams of "Mummy isn't here to wipe your tears away now!" rang out from the training staff, and their spit hit our faces as they stood nose to nose with us wailing like screaming banshees.

This sort of treatment is aimed to weed out the weak, after all we were applying to join the army and not the local florists. Growing up where I did I very quickly became accustomed to this abusive behaviour and just shut my brain off to it, several of the other potential recruits were not able to shut it out so easily though, and a few came apart at the seams and were rejected within the first hour, they were taken away with their tales between their legs. 30 had become 25 before we had even left the parade ground.

The first half of the day consisted of watching videos of life in the army; none of which showed the exotic locations promised in the newspaper advert that I previously saw, and interviews trying to find out if we excelled or showed promise in any particular area, such as engineering. Then came the fitness tests.

We were taken to a gymnasium and paired up with other potential recruits, we were then put through a set of tests such as push-up, and pull-up. Although slightly strenuous I found these quite easy, working in an engineering factory I had built up good upper body strength from lifting heavy steel bars all day. Then we were taken outside for the 1.5 mile B.F.T.

The 1.5 mile route took us around part of the camp's perimeter fence and through barrack blocks that were being used by the Paras (parachute regiment). When the P.T.I (Physical Training Instructor) blew the whistle to start the test I found myself being drawn into a pace I had never ran at before, everybody just went flat out. I knew at the time going fast early in any run is a stupid thing to do and it spells trouble for you later on, however I didn't want to get left behind and be singled out by the training staff as a "back of the pack jack." So I put my head down and sprinted on, after a few minutes though the all too familiar feelings of breathless exhaustion were kicking in, much like the first time I tried to run on the school training track. I started to worry so I slowed my pace. At first my heart sank and I thought I would appear rubbish to the staff with all the others runners leaving me for dust. However this wasn't the case, after another minute or so I started catching up and passing the other would-be recruits, they had all gone out way too fast and were struggling to keep going.

The route we took had no distance markers so we didn't know exactly how far we had left to run, also we had our watches taken off us at the start of the day, so it was only guess work in our minds just how long we had been running for. As we approached the Paras accommodation barracks we were subjected to a barrage of profanity and abusive encouragement, I was largely overlooked as I ran through this section as their shouts were directed at the runners who were now struggling for breath.

When I rounded a corner and saw that I was finally on the straight bit of road that lead to the finish, I upped my pace again and gave it my all to the line. As we each crossed the line we were roughly dragged over to a wall and lined up in the order in which we had finished, I was 4th out of the 25 that had started. Several of the other lads were bending over and falling to their knees out of breath, but they were man handled back up right and screamed at to stay standing.

They didn't tell us at that moment if we had passed or failed, or what our run finish time was, only later when we had our last interview telling us if we had passed the weekend or not, did I learn I had ran the B.F.T in 9 minutes 8 seconds, a time that could have qualified me for the parachute regiment, I was stunned. I passed the weekend with flying colours and I couldn't stop smiling to myself on the train back to Coventry.

March of 1994 I signed the oath of allegiance and officially became a recruit in the British Army, basic training was the only thing that stood in my way from becoming a soldier.

Chapter 2

Basic Training

Late May 1994 I found myself stood outside the gates of Bassingbourn Barracks, near Royston in Hertfordshire. Back then it was where new recruits from several infantry regiments, including the Royal Regiment of Fusiliers, did their 10 weeks basic training. For me it was a very worrying and exciting time. Worrying because I didn't truly know what was in store for me, and exciting because it was a change from my mundane existence in Coventry.

The first few days of training were a hellish blur of being issued our combat equipment and shown how to care for it. Then learning how to do mind numbing chores, from how to polish your parade boots to a mirror shine, to making the sheets on our beds with hospital corners, and pulling them so tight that you could bounce a 2 pence coin off them like a trampoline, and catch it again.

At the time I couldn't see the point in all these pointless chores, how the hell did folding my bed a certain way teach me how to be a good soldier? When I think back now though, I know they were teaching us the principle of how to be tenacious in doing a single task until perfection was achieved.

Eventually we got around to doing our first basic training runs, these were a bit of a chaotic mess at first as we were told to run as a 3 rank platoon. Many of us would stumble over each other as the faster recruits would kick the heels of those in front. The corporals in charge of our training were brutal and we all got punished badly in the first few days until we mastered running as a unit.

The first runs we did were only around 2 miles in distance as the training staff built up our fitness. We also did the B.F.T again, however I was a lot slower this time and only achieved a time of 10 minutes 12 seconds, a full minute slower than when I was at the test weekend. I put this down to the fact that we did it on an airfield this time and I could see how far I had left to the finish, and I didn't have the pressure of passing it to be selected.

After a couple of weeks all of our fitness improved, and those who couldn't keep up with the overall progress of the platoon, either got back-trooped (made to go back and start basic training again with a new platoon), or D.A.O.R (Discharge as of Right) - They quit.

We saw our platoon drop in number from 32 down to 26 in those first 2 weeks alone, and with a further 8 weeks left until we passed out of training we knew we would lose more.

The ones who suffered the most were the lads from Gibraltar regiment, who also did their training at Bassingbourne. They were used to living in the heat of the south of Spain, and found the British climate far too chilly for their liking. This reached a peak on week 3 when we did our first field exercise, it was only a 24 hour affair of us doing patrols in a wooded area and setting up camp for the night. It may have been early June, but the night of that exercise we experienced a very hard ground frost, it was torturous to me, for the Gibraltar lads it was too much, and a few of them could be heard crying in the early hours while they were out on look out, watching for a potential enemy.

The corporals heard this and threw a mock attack at our camp in the early hours. Thunder flashes lit up the trees and automatic gun fire rang out in the misty night air. It may have only been blank ammunition being fired, but for us new recruits it was no less frightening than if live rounds were going off. This simulated attack caused massive confusion for all of us as a platoon, we were nowhere near trained enough to deal with such an eventuality, and absolute chaos ensued. I and another lad next to me managed to stand-to and put down fire in the direction of the attack, however many of the other lads in the platoon couldn't find their rifles in the dark, the hands of the lads from Gibraltar were so cold they couldn't grip the cocking handles on their rifles to make them ready to fire, and one other recruit couldn't undo his sleeping bag due to the zip being frozen solid, he was found crawling in it like a giant caterpillar through the darkness.

We all had a huge telling off for the complete carnage that the exercise had become, yet we all learned many lessons from it, most importantly the value of looking after each other.

As the weeks progressed the training runs became more intense, we upped our miles to 5, then 8, and we were also subjected to "challenges" while we were on these runs, from having to do the camp assault course at the beginning and end of each run, to carrying heavy and awkward items such as logs. On one occasion I found myself carrying an ironing board around on exercise because I was caught moaning about my evening chores; it became very interesting trying to take cover and conceal myself in woodland with a giant surfboard shaped item strapped to my back.

Eventually we went from running in training shoes to doing it in our combat boots, then carrying our Bergen's (British military rucksack) loaded with our equipment. After a few weeks of training like this we were subjected to another test called the C.F.T (Combat Fitness Test), which required us to carry 25kgs on an 8 mile route, and it was to be completed in under 2 hours. This was where I found my true calling. As I have mentioned earlier I was never fast, yet I took to load carrying like a fish to water, I don't know why as I am not a large or powerfully built person, yet I found carrying weight (or at least this weight) quite easy, maybe it was just the slower pace, either way I was far suited to this style of training.

When carrying a heavy load over large distances it is not practical to run, for one you will tire quickly, and secondly in the military it doesn't pay to make a lot of noise or you make yourself a target. So when loaded up with equipment we vary our pace, from speed marching to slow jogging and back again as we progressed; this is called Tabbing (T.A.B – Tactical Advance to Battle), it prepares soldiers for carrying heavy kit and equipment over long distances within a certain time frame.

We all started the C.F.T in 3 ranks as usual, the first couple of miles literally flew by for me and I personally found the going quite easy, however a few of my fellow recruits were struggling, and by the half way point some were coming unglued big time. Screams and shouts from the training staff couldn't even motivate them to keep up and subsequently we left many in our wake as we progressed. This really surprised me as some of the fastest and what I thought fittest recruits, the ones who excelled at the B.F.T, were struggling with the load carrying. We obviously all have our niche, and this was mine.

Coming towards the end of this test I found myself in an all-out sprint to the finish with 3 other lads, I crossed the line first, and was so proud of myself, it was hard to believe I had been close to collapse after 1 lap of the school training track a few months earlier, yet here I was sprinting after an 8 mile load carry. One of the training staff even patted me on the back, yet as it is with the dark humour of the military he had to throw in a witty comment, "Well-done Fusilier, let's see if you're that enthusiastic when you're running towards a real enemy."

From this moment forward my confidence soared. My once shy, mild and meek nature that made me a target for bullies in my younger years changed too. I started to realise I could overcome anything physically or mentally if I put in enough effort and gave it my all. Many in the civilian world who look in on a military life only see the brutality of it, they see recruits being screamed at, and them scrambling over assault courses, but unless you have experienced it first-hand you will not understand. For some the level of discipline needed is crushing and they fold quickly, others find it easier and can just go with its flow, they focus not fold. I focused.

I must say though that when you do eventually leave the military after being up against fellow soldiers and leaders with strong heads, it is very hard to let anybody tell you what to do again, especially those who have gained a position of power in a company and have no respect for their employees. My experiences in the military made me very head strong, some would call me a stubborn bastard, but the military taught me to treat people the same as they treat me, if they showed me little or no respect, then they get none in return. This has caused several conflicts over the years when I returned to civilian working life, so much so I could write another book about it. Anyway that was in the future for me at this time, and my military life was just beginning.

Basic training continued and so did the brutality of it, on top of the running we spent many long hours in the gym doing pull-ups, sit-ups, rope climbing, circuit training, anything they could throw at us. Some evenings, if it had been raining, we would all be marched over to a nearby woodland, there was a shallow stream that ran through this wooded area and a tree had fallen across this stream. Us recruits would be randomly paired up to stand on this tree and fight each other until one of us fell off into the muddy water below; this may sound brutal in its nature, however it taught us balance, patience, and more importantly standing up and facing an adversary. There was no faking a fall and finishing the battle early, if the instructors thought we gave up without giving our all then we would be put back on the tree to fight again, and again, until they were happy. Needless to say many injuries occurred along the way, but nothing too serious.

Me during army basic training, 1994

There was only one time I really suffered in basic training, and it was completely my own fault. We were on our final field exercise, it was a 2 day simulated invasion in a military testing area called Yardley Chase, in Northamptonshire. We were tasked with digging in (setting up camp), securing a perimeter, and then sending out patrols to find the enemy (another platoon on exercise with us).

It all started off well, we had all progressed as a platoon and had developed our skills since our disastrous first exercise. Whereas we had frost on the first exercise, we had blistering

July heat on this one, with scorching sunshine in the day and it was incredibly humid at night. Yardley Chase is an area of low lying grass land, swamps, and wooded areas, and in this hot weather it was covered in a cloud of biting midges. Although we all had insect repellent on, we were being eaten alive. After a full day of this and trying to focus on our duties, tempers grew thin and several of us started snapping at each other.

This reached a peak for me at 1:30am when I was out on a 6 man patrol. We were crossing a small ridge just below its crest to avoid being a silhouette against the star filled sky, when I felt another in my patrol (I'll call him D) brush his boots against the back of mine. When out on patrol we were taught to keep our spacing between each other, to make us a harder and wider target to hit should we be seen, or should one of us set off an explosive device such as a landmine, it wouldn't take us all out.

I instantly turned around and whispered in an angry voice for him to keep his distance. D whose temper was obviously on edge too told me to speed up, however I was 3rd in line and my speed was dictated by the man in front of me. I turned to continue and as I did so D pushed me on the shoulder. I saw red! I lifted up my left elbow and slammed it into his face. He instantly retaliated and threw a punch at me that caught me in the side of my head. We both threw our rifles down and started having a full blown fight right there in the open. We were rolling around on the grass pummelling each other when out of the darkness an instructor came over and started kicking us both in the ribs. He ripped us apart and threatened us with a spell in military jail for such reckless behaviour in a simulated warzone.

I look back on this incident now and I am quite ashamed I let my temper get the better of me in that situation, however I was only 19 years old at the time and not as well controlled emotionally.

We patrolled back to our woodland camp accompanied by the instructor who intervened, and told we would be dealt with after the exercise. As morning approached rain began to fall. At first it was welcome as it suppressed the biting insects, but then it became intense. I fished my waterproof gear out of my Bergen but in doing so accidentally dropped my issue fleece/jumper into a large puddle. The jumper acted like a sponge and instantly soaked up a huge amount of water. At that moment we were told to bug-out (pack up camp and move quickly), I was forced to ram this now heavy wet jumper back in my Bergen, as I did this I failed to make my Bergen water tight again.

As we started moving the weight on my back went from uncomfortable to absolutely crushing. I didn't know it at the time but I had left a gap open at the top of my pack and it was acting as a rain collector, filling my entire Bergen up and soaking into all my equipment. We also had 240 rounds of blank ammunition on each of us for our rifles, it felt like I had a horse sat on my shoulders and after an hour of marching I was a broken man, but I refused to complain to the instructors as I was already in their bad books from the fight incident. Just when I thought things couldn't get any worse the instructors simulated a gas attack. I was in a state of semi-comprehension when the words "GAS! GAS! GAS!" rang out.

I fell to my knees in the mud, took my helmet off, and quickly retrieved my respirator from a pouch on my right hip. I put it on, made sure it was sealed correctly and replaced my helmet back on my head. We continued on in the pouring rain for another 20 minutes or so like this before I finally collapsed. The insane weight of my pack, now accompanied by my inability to get enough oxygen in my system through my respirator, became too much, and I went face down in the mud.

Two instructors came over, sat me up right, ripped my helmet and respirator off and started checking me, it was only when they started taking my pack off that they realised the true problem. One of them tried to lift it then shouted out, "What the hell have you got in there my boy? Gold fucking bars?!"

He held my pack upside down and all my equipment fell out accompanied by many litres of rain water. They rammed a chocolate bar down my throat to make sure I had at least some form of food energy in my system, then instructed me to repack all of my equipment and make sure my pack was waterproof this time. I was there on my hands and knees in the mud, rain smashing down around me and I was repacking my Bergen, yes my gear was now covered in mud and wet, but at least I wasn't carrying a swimming pool too.

With the water in my pack gone the load felt substantially lighter and I recovered much of my strength. I caught back up to the rest of the platoon and made it to the end of the exercise. When I saw the 4 tonner truck waiting to take us back to base I literally cried, this was the first time I had truly been physically broken, it would not be the last.

A few days later I was taken in to see my commanding officer about the fight incident that happened on exercise, I was stood to attention expecting a harsh punishment or even dismissal, when he told me to relax and stand easy. He then went on to tell me that he had heard nothing but good things about me from my training instructors, he told me I was the perfect recruit and showed amazing promise. I was at a loss for words. He then dismissed me, as I turned to march out of his office he said "Oh, and if someone pisses you off on patrol in future, do try to make it back to a secure location before thumping them." He then turned to his desk and waved me away with a sweep of his hand.

I passed out of basic training shortly after this, the sun blazed down from a clear blue sky as we all marched across the parade ground and received our blessing from the R.S.M (Regimental Sergeant Major). Now that basic training was completed, it was time to specialise in our trade craft, although I was in an infantry regiment I made it clear quite early on that I was interested in training as a medic. As with other topics in my life I could continue and go through my entire military career here, however that too is for another book, this story is about running and endurance, so I shall continue to my next venture in that. It happened several years later, after I had left the army and moved back to Coventry…………..

Chapter 3

Burning Bridges

I returned to Coventry a completely changed person than when I had left, I had a confidence about myself that I never had before. The place was much the same, the neighbourhood where my parents still lived had changed little, and the same run down flats were visible on the horizon with their windows boarded up. However the fear I had of the area was gone. I used to cower away when a group of young lads would walk towards me, now I refused to be intimidated by their behaviour.

Although I had become a qualified medic, I opted to go back to doing engineering work in factories. Back in the late 90s Coventry was still at the pinnacle of car production, many major companies had their production plants there; Peugeot, Jaguar and Land Rover, all had a hold on the city and a large number of the parts for their cars were made in Coventry's factories. It paid better to work in manufacturing rather than health care.

Going back to factory work after spending time in the armed forces is a very hard thing to do, for me it was soul destroying. In the military your opinions and experience are valued, in a factory they are not. No matter how much experience you have, or how many years you have worked in the same place, your opinions are of zero importance to managers who are there only to make money. To them you are nothing but an ant in a nest, a drone in a hive, a cog in a machine that can be replaced at will. In the military your opinions are valued, your experience is everything and even the highest ranking officer will take on board what those below him have to say to achieve a given goal.

Needless to say going back to being treated like dirt caused (and continues to cause) a few issues. I found myself nose to nose with those in charge, refusing to bow to their threatening behaviour. Some people interpreted this as me trying to be "tough," and they saw me as a troublemaker. Very few could see it was the attitude of those in charge that provoked my reactions. As I have said in the previous chapter I will always treat people how they treat me. Treat me badly and expect nothing else but that in return.

I used to blow away all of the stress of work by going for an evening run, which was an interesting affair where I lived, as being on the streets at night was not advised, especially with the roaming gangs. This for me added to the excitement, as it would make me run faster. There were many times when I was out running that I would find a police car flashing its lights at me with its blues whirling away on top. They would assume I was running from a crime and take to body searching me. They always appeared surprised when I told them I was out doing a training run, as not many people ran for recreation in my neighbourhood.

One night I was out running and on the return route to my parents' house, when two lads stepped out from a block of garages I was passing. I came to a stop expecting some kind of confrontation (I had experienced many by this point and used to just outrun those who tried it on), this time however one produced a knife and the other a handgun. To this day I do not know if the gun was real, fake, or just an air pistol, but if you don't know you should always treat it as if it were the real thing.

They asked me for money, I replied that I didn't go out running with any. They then told me to show them where I lived. Obviously I was not willing to take them to my parents' house, so I started to lead them back the way I had come. After several paces I bolted between two parked cars and sprinted off down a side alley. They tried to pursue me but to no avail, I lost them quickly.

After taking a huge detour to ensure I wasn't followed, I went back home. My confidence that was unbreakable for so long was starting to crack again; it had been a very long time since I had felt scared, but seeing that gun pointed at me, whether it was fake or real, caused me to worry. I had heard of many murders on the news in Coventry over the years, and I didn't want to become another statistic.

I informed the police about the incident, and they filed a report, but the police officers that interviewed me about it said they had 20 reports like this on a daily basis in the city, and

I was lucky I got away injury free. My parents were very upset about what happened, and in an attempt to stop causing them anymore distress I ceased running in the evenings. I relied on running, it was my escapism, it helped me cope with the stress of work, and not doing it crushed my spirit even further and started me on a downwards spiral.

I soon found myself spending my evenings drinking in the local pub to pass the time, what started out as a couple of beers each night, soon progressed to many, and the weeks fast turned into months. The strong, confident me was ebbing away and being replaced by a slump shouldered figure who slouched at the bar.

I still stayed in touch with many of my friends that I had in school and grown up with, however they had all started taking their own paths in life, some had families now, some had moved away, others had turned to crime and even died in their pursuit of it, and here I was in limbo.

I tried several times to break this pointless routine, eventually I did it by working behind the bar from which I had been drinking from. I would finish my day job then tend the bar in the evenings. This was a true eye opener, only when you are on the other side of the bar looking out do you truly see just how chaotic and mindless drinking to stupidity can be. While drinking I never really paid much attention to how many fights used to break out in the place, as I had my back to them and never got involved. But when it's your job to help look after the place they seem to happen every half an hour.

I was working behind the bar one summer afternoon, the sun was blazing in through the windows illuminating the bar, several old people were playing darts, others were sat at tables, and in the middle of the floor there were two locals grappling and rolling around getting each other in headlocks, and beating each other senseless.

Normally I'd try to break them up and call for the landlord or bouncers from the back lounge, however this time I just left them to it, I let them knock the crap out of each other and I didn't care. I had finally snapped, I looked around and in that very moment I literally said out loud "fuck this!" I dropped what I was doing and walked out. I had finally had enough, I couldn't take this mindless existence anymore.

I went home that night and told my parents that I planned to move away – instantly. They seemed slightly confused by what I was saying, if anything I don't think they believed me.

The following morning I crammed my car with as many of my belongings as I could fit in it, filled the fuel tank up, and drove out of Coventry. I hit the motorway and just headed south. I had no clear vision of where I was heading, but I sure knew where I didn't want to be, and that was Coventry.

The further I drove away from the place the happier I became, I hadn't felt this excited about the future since I first entered the army careers office all those years ago. I had tried to escape from Coventry once, this time I had to make it permanent, I swore that no matter what happened or where I ended up I would not return to that city to live ever again. Some bridges you have to burn, to stop you from returning to where you should never have been in the first place, and this was one of those bridges.

Just after 2pm on August 5th 2000 I arrived in Plymouth. I drove through the small city and navigated my way to the waterfront, parked my car by the citadel on the Hoe, and walked out to look at the sea. It was a glorious day, the sun sparkled off the glass flat water like diamonds, naval ships were anchored near the breakwater, and small yachts darted around on the gentle breeze. After spending so long gazing upon the boarded up windows of flats and the graffiti lined streets of my old neighbourhood, this truly was a glimpse of heaven, and I instantly fell in love with the place.

Having nowhere to live didn't bother me at all, I was just glad to be away from the chains that had been holding my spirit in a dungeon for so long. For the first week I slept in my car, then I bought a tent and pitched up in a local campsite. Plymouth, and the South West in general, struggles to find skilled workers in the engineering and manufacturing sectors, so getting a job was easy, and I secured one within a few days.

I phoned my parents, brothers, and friends back home on a regular basis, and many of them thought I was mad for just upping and leaving like I did. They also expected me to return to Coventry sooner or later with my tail between my legs. This gave me more determination than ever to succeed. I have always found the best thing that motivates me to achieve a goal is to be told that I cannot do it, I love to prove people wrong in those situations.

Within a couple of months I had moved out of the campsite where I was staying and into a flat near Plymouth University. The accommodation was poor, and the locals who were mostly students, partied until the early hours. It wasn't the dream existence I had hoped for when I first left Coventry, but at least there was much less chance of being shot at.

With the streets less dangerous than my previous neighbourhood up north I got back into running again. In the evenings I would jog from where I lived, out to the waterfront and back, it felt exhilarating to be able to run carefree again, and not be looking out for would-be assassins along the way.

As my fitness came back I took to doing longer and longer routes, and I started to explore parts of this new city I now called home.

Being Plymouth is a naval city with an extensive history in both warfare and exploration, it is impossible to travel any distance around its streets without encountering something maritime related, be that monuments dedicated to those who lost their lives during the great wars, or statues of pioneers of old, such as Sir Francis Drake.

Plymouth is also home to Her Majesty's Naval Base, Devonport (HMNB Devonport). It is one of three operating bases in the U.K. for the Royal Navy, and is the largest naval base in Western Europe. It also houses an impressive fleet, including (at the time) the largest vessel in the Royal Navy, HMS

Ocean. Along with this, Plymouth also has two Royal Marine Commando units permanently stationed, 42 Commando at Bickleigh Barracks, and 29 Commando Regiment Royal Artillery, whose garrison is in the Royal Citadel on the Hoe. There are also two Territorial Army commando units (troops) in the city too.

It was while I was out running one evening that I encountered some of the troops from one of these territorial units training. I was exploring a new wooded area north of the city and they were out tabbing in their combat gear. The instant I saw them I had this flashback to my basic training days, it wasn't a negative or bad image: it was one of pride. Whenever my mind drifted back to basic training I never thought of the pain I went through, I only ever remembered the feeling of elation whenever I had completed a run or task.

I continued on running but I could not get the image of them training out of my head. I realised I missed doing that, pushing myself, feeling part of a tight unit whose members trusted each other implicitly, and the camaraderie of it all.

The following day I found myself phoning the local TA (Territorial Army) centre arranging an interview. I was 26 years of age by this point, and even though that is young in the civilian world, it is middle aged in the military world. When I met the OC (Officer Commanding) of the TA unit I was applying for he made it clear that my age could well be an issue, after all it wasn't just any Territorial Army unit I was joining, it was attached to 3 Commando Brigade, which meant I would have to complete the All Arms Commando Course(AACC). Normally the AACC lasts for 13 weeks and is run by the Royal Marines at the Commando Training Centre Royal Marines (CTCRM), Lympstone. However the TA runs a slightly different programme where a recruit would do several build up weekends of preparation, before going to Lympstone to complete the last 2 weeks of the course, which has all of the final tests to see if you have what it takes to earn the coveted green beret and commando dagger.

The OC made it perfectly clear that it was substantially harder for a person to pass the AACC at my age and doing it through a TA unit, because I would have to train myself to the high standard required while still working in a full time job. I however would not be put off, if anything I wanted to prove everybody wrong again and show them that it could be done with enough determination.

The OC could see my determination and he said he was happy for me to join the troop, as long as I could pass the entry fitness tests. These tests were almost identical to my army entrance tests, the only difference were the number of repetitions needed in some exercises and the speed of the B.F.T. So I knew the requirement needed of me instantly. I had a month before I was tested, so I went home that afternoon and started upping my training in preparation.

I stopped using my car and started running to work, much like I did all those years ago in Coventry, however I now had far more pleasant scenery on my commute in and home, running alongside Plymouth's Embankment Road, to the views of the river Plym. I had to build my upper body strength up again too, so I joined a gym, but trying to keep a set routine going while others trained around me was impossible, I could never get on the equipment I needed. To get around this problem, I bought a simple weight bench, and a dumbbell and bar bell set, which I set up in my flat.

I trained twice a day, every day for the month leading up to the fitness tests, and I ate everything I could. Even when I wasn't hungry I would graze on food to try to build myself up and repair my body from my constant training.

In that time I was issued with all my combat gear. This equipment was far superior to what I had been given in the regular army, and we were free to adapt it any way we liked, which made load carrying even easier. I went to the TA centre on Wednesday evenings for that month and got to know the lads in the troop. I hit it off with almost all of them, there were two troopers however who were full of themselves and thought themselves a cut above the rest, I have encountered several people like this over the years attached to military units and that sort of bad attitude can bring down morale.

I tried to get on with this sour pair, but no matter what I did they just tried to cause problems for me and everybody in general, so I eventually just ignored them. My story about them is far from over though, as I went on to have several run-ins with them in the future.

When the day of my fitness tests came I was more fired up than ever and I absolutely annihilated them, far exceeding even my own expectations. Even the B.F.T. I managed to get in little over 10 minutes. The OC was very impressed and he shook my hand and welcomed me to the troop. I then found myself signing the Oath of Allegiance for the second time in my life. I was now officially back in a military unit, but little did I realise at the time just what adventures I would have with this TA troop, and how much pain and hard work I would have to go through on my journey through the All Arms Commando Course.

Chapter 4

Going Commando

It felt fantastic being back in such a tight group again. I would look forward to my Wednesday evenings when the troop would get together for training up at the TA centre. Almost all of what we were being taught in the lecture rooms I knew already from my regular army days, yet it was nice to refresh and recap on a lot of the theory, plus technology had advanced some since my old days in the forces, and I had to catch up on these developments.

Physical training, however, was very intense, far more so than back in my early army days. These guys were relentless, they didn't train in the conventional way with set running courses; they would literally get us in one of the 4 tonner military trucks, or the back of a mini bus, drive us miles away from the TA centre and tell us to run back to it as quickly as we could. One time it was a good 15 miles away. I was kicked out the back of the truck on a deserted country lane and told that I had 2 hours to get back to the TA centre. As hard as these training runs were, they were great fun, and a brilliant personal challenge.

I started going away with the unit on weekends too, and it was on these weekends that I realised the troop also had a taste for the amber nectar. Not only could they train hard, boy could they drink hard too.

Now, I used to consume a few beers when I had my low point in Coventry, but the level of drinking this troop did was on a biblical scale. They were never rowdy or caused any trouble, they just drank, A LOT! Yet they would always be up fresh the following morning ready for a training run.

My first true weekend away with them was at Weymouth on the Dorset coast. There were approximately 15 of us, plus 3 NCOs (Non-commissioned officers - training staff). We arrived at Chickerell Training Camp, in the back of a mini bus, on a sunny Friday evening in August. The air was warm, the sky was clear, and I felt fantastic.

We were given zero instruction of what the weekend would entail, however I was expecting an evening of getting my gear ready for some form of training exercise the following morning. How wrong I was. Within a few minutes of arriving we were told by our Staff Sergeant to drop our gear, dress casual, grab our wallets, and all meet by the mini bus in 10 minutes.

When assembled and back on board the bus, we were driven out of the camp without a word being spoken by those in charge, but when I looked around at the rest of the troopers, they all had knowing smiles on their faces. I whispered a question to the lad next to me that I got on well with, asking what was in store, and he replied with the simple answer "Training exercise, don't lose your wallet."

The sun began to set and darkness crept in as our small bus continued on. I paid little attention to where we were heading, it was just endless narrow country lanes. Only when darkness was truly taking hold did the bus stop. Then the Staff Sergeant called out the name of one of my fellow troopers, this lad promptly leapt from his seat and went to the front of the bus. He was then given a small laminated map and told to get out.

We drove on again for a few minutes and this procedure happened again, another person would be selected, given a map, and be sent out of the door.

After 7 troopers had departed this way my name was called out. I went to the front of the bus slightly confused about what was actually going on. Like the others I was given an A4 sized map, scale 1:50000, with a red arrow pointed at a location in the top left hand corner of it.

I looked up from the map and asked the Staff Sergeant what it was for. He was a small man in his mid-40s, with little round rimmed spectacles that stood on the end of his nose. He gazed at me over the top of his glasses and replied "It's for finding the pub."

I said that I didn't know where I was on the map, so how could I find the place in question if I didn't know my start point. He breathed a sigh and said "If you found yourself behind enemy lines, do you think you would know your location in relation to a possible extraction point? Well that is the purpose of this exercise. Use your ingenuity. Also, you are not allowed to ask any civilians for help."

I stepped off the mini bus into the dark cool night air. I was down a country lane with high hedgerows that obscured my view of the surrounding area, the stars were bright in the heavens above, and the only man made illumination I could see were distant street lights back down the lane from which we had driven.

The bus pulled away and I watched the tail end of it disappear into the night, and as the hum of its engine faded into insignificance, I could make out the sound of the sea, gentle waves lapping a shore line.

Having no light to see the map, I took off back down the road towards the street lights. When I arrived there, I studied the map, and then orientated it so that the shoreline on the map corresponded to the direction I could hear the sea from. I looked at the red arrow indicating where I needed to get to in relation to the shore line. The arrow pointed to a location some way in land, and I was at a point on the coast which covered about 2 miles in length on the map. I had no compass and no mobile phone back then. So I decided to head back along the country lane until I encountered some dwellings.

I ran for about a mile before I started seeing small cottages and outhouses dotted along the road. I was tempted to knock on the doors to ask my exact location, however I remembered the Staff Sergeant's instructions forbidding me to do that. I continued on and plunged back into darkness again.

Then I came to a cross roads, where there was a small road which lead towards the coast, and another one heading inland. I opted to go inland as the red arrow on the map was well away from the shore line.

I plodded on for around 15 minutes in pure darkness before I encountered a small group of quaint country houses with thatched roofs; there was a dainty shop that was closed, and a small bridge leaping over a stream. This little hamlet caught in the halo cast by the street lights, was a true picture of bliss. I stopped for a moment to take in the scene, the place looked wonderful, and it was only the presence of a modern day telephone box next to the tiny bridge that ruined it all.

Then I was struck by an idea. I ran over to the phone box, picked up the receiver and dialled 100 for the operator. The female voice on the other end of the line asked for my enquiry, I said "This is going to sound strange, but can you tell me the grid reference of this telephone box please?"

At first, I was met with silence, I then went on to say that I was lost. The operator asked me if I would like to be put through to the police, but I insisted that I was fine, and that I was in fact a hiker who had become slightly disorientated and was looking for my campsite, however I had a map and just needed to know my location. She then relented and read off the 6 digit grid reference of the phone box I was in, I quickly located it on the map under the glow of the street lights, and I was off again.

Now I knew where I was, I could easily pick the quickest route to the red arrow on the map. Within an hour, I found myself going through the door to an old country tavern. It was a quiet little pub with an old hard wooden bar warped by age and tended to by an elderly couple. There were a few locals scattered around the place, and hidden away in the shadows at the far corner were a group of individuals, whispering over a table. They were the members of my troop doing the best they could to blend in to the background.

I approached their table and the staff sergeant turned to me with a smile on his face. He then pipped up "Well done, you've passed the first test. Now go and get yourself a drink. In fact you best make it two or three, it's only an hour until the place closes."

We all arrived back at the camp around midnight, and most of the guys were decidedly wobbly on their feet. Everybody crashed out on their respective beds, and after what literally felt like the blink of an eye, it was 6am and they were all getting up and heading off for breakfast in the camp canteen.

While sat at breakfast with the rest of the troop, I enquired as to what was in store for the day; we were now accompanied by the OC who had driven through the night and recently arrived at the camp. He lazily said through a mouth full of bacon and sausage that we were going for a bike ride, and that we were to dress in some casual P.T. (Physical Training) kit.

Obviously we hadn't travelled over from Plymouth with any bicycles so I assumed we would be provided with some adequately cared for machines to see us through the day's activities. Shortly after breakfast we were taken to a large shed to be issued with our bikes. Well they resembled bikes anyway. They were a collection of mountain bikes from the dark ages; to say they were well used would be a gross understatement. They had rusty chains, the wheels were caked in mud, and the frames were as thick as scaffold poles and weighed a ton.

As I took possession of mine and attempted to push it some distance away to inspect it, I heard a scrapping sound: it was the back tyre dragging. The wheel refused to turn due to the brakes being stuck on with rust. This was not the well cared for machine I had anticipated receiving. This was a very sad and abused contraption, and I'm sure that if it had eyes it would have cried.

I located a maintenance shed and used what tools I could find to release the stuck brakes. I also gave all moving parts a good oil and tried to get everything moving again. It still sounded like a wood saw trying to cut through sheet steel, but at least the wheels now turned.

Happy now that I had a working form of transport I joined the others, whose bikes were in the same state of disrepair as mine. Then the OC turned up pushing a state of the art piece of precision cycling engineering. This thing sparkled like a chandelier in a ballroom. Its stainless steel, aluminium and chrome framework were a glorious display of modern cycling technology crafted into a dart driven by the legs.

Then I looked down at my sorry excuse for a ride; it resembled a large sideways diamond constructed of rusty scaffold poles, with 2 wheels at each end and a seat on top. It was like comparing a formula 1 race car to a Lada.

Yet again we were told to bring our wallets as we would stop off for something to eat along the way. I was starting to think this was more of a jolly few days away rather than a military training weekend.

Then the OC, who was now dressed in what appeared to be Olympic style cycling gear, turned and said to us all "Right, I'll lead the way. We will go through the village and then we will be heading off road. Do try to keep up."

We went through the camp gates in a long line. Our little convoy snaked through the narrow streets of the small village that surrounded the camp, then we went out on to country lanes. Keeping up was hard right from the start. While the OC's bike was as light as air and he stormed ahead, the rest of us felt like we were towing trailers loaded with bricks, and we had to stand on our pedals and sway from side to side to get any form of momentum going.

After about 20 minutes, we came to a kissing gate that lead out into some fields. The OC then informed us that the rest of the ride would be off road, and quite hilly. This last statement was a pure lie, it wasn't hilly at all: it was nothing short of mountainous!

For the next 3 hours, we all ascended and descended dirt tracks that can only be described as near vertical. Many times, we all had to get off our bikes and carry them over shale and rocky outcrops. It became totally exhausting. The OC however just threw his bike on his shoulder like it was a fashion accessory and danced across whatever obstacle he encountered like a ballerina. He was in his element, and I'm sure he secretly enjoyed gazing back on all of us struggling, dragging our contraptions like condemned men going to their slaughter.

The only break we got was when we encountered a country pub out in the wilds. It was another thatched roof affair with a beer garden dotted with wooden benches. I dropped my bike and literally collapsed on one of the benches with my face down on the table in front of me. I was suddenly brought out of my dream state by a jolt on my head. I looked up to see a pint of beer and a Cornish pasty on a plate. The OC said "Get that down you son, and we'll be on our way."

The last thing I wanted in the world was beer at that time. I was dehydrated and physically ruined. However I went with the flow and wolfed the lot down my gullet. After exhausting myself so much, the beer went straight to my head, and I felt light on my feet. The pasty was very much needed though. Before we set off I bought 2 bottles of water from the pub and some crisps, which I put in the small pack I had on my back.

We were back off again, and continued to be led over the worst possible terrain, from bolder fields to boggy marshes. It was relentless. After a further 4 hours we eventually saw the distant perimeter of the camp again, its fence reminiscent of prisons the world over. I, however, was very glad to return to this one.

When I finally dismounted off my bike, I was completely destroyed, both physically and mentally. The OC, still on his bike, sat there like a proud cowboy straddling his steed. He scanned us from behind his mirror shades, smiled and said "Well done chaps, the GPS says we have covered 80 miles today. Give your legs a rest now. You'll need them again in the morning." He then cycled in a tight circle and disappeared at lightning speed across the camp.

As we returned our bikes to the storage shed, we encountered our Staff Sergeant. He was as full of energy as ever and shot a beaming smile at us. He cheerfully said "Get yourself showered and cleaned up lads. We're heading into Weymouth in an hour for a few drinks."

These few drinks turned into 6 hours of relentless pub crawls, which ended up at a night club. I drank water and soft drinks for most of this time as I needed to rehydrate from the onslaught of the day. I do not know how most of the other troop members could just carry on drinking alcohol like they did after such a physically savage day.

It was 2am when we all eventually left the night club and headed back to the camp. I was in a daze. Yet again my head had barely touched the pillow before I found myself being awoken by the hustle and bustle of the others preparing for breakfast. I had only managed 3 hours sleep at best.

I shuffled off to the canteen, legs stiff and sore from the previous day's ride. I noticed many of the others too were sporting an awkward gait, and no doubt feeling their aches. As we munched our beans and bacon, the OC arrived in his running shorts and t-shirt. He was as fresh as a daisy and far too enthusiastic for my liking. He told us to eat what we could, as we were going for a little jog in an hours' time.

Although I felt rough, I thought a "little jog" would loosen me up and blow away the sleepy cobwebs clouding my mind. Yet again I was wrong, because the OC's version of a "little jog" was a brutal route from the camp in Chickerell, through Weymouth, out to Portland Bill lighthouse, and back again.

We all did this as a group, and trying to think back on that run now I only get fragmented memories, because I shut my mind down most of the way around it. I don't know how many miles it was, maybe 10 or 12, but I suffered for every single one of them.

By the time we returned to camp a few hours later I was close to needing hospital treatment. I could hardly stand, but I refused to show the other members of the troop just how much I was suffering. This was my first weekend away with the troop and I wanted to prove to them that I could keep up with their pace and fit in, although deep down I doubted that I could.

That weekend was the first taster of what my life would become, a blur of endless endurance challenges and military exercises. My days were rammed. I would spend 8 hours in my full time job during the weekdays, and every evening training or sorting my kit out. On Wednesdays I would train up at the TA centre for 3 hours, where I studied everything from counter terrorism to arctic warfare. Most weekends I would spend away with the troop, either doing field exercises out on Dartmoor or Woodbury Common, or another version of my first weekend away, where we would do several physical challenges intermixed with drinking sessions. It was tough, but I really enjoyed it, plus it started to get me passionate about adventure racing, and trying to get to locations by any means available.

I was still training towards doing the AACC, and waiting to be accepted into the next available slot for it. One Wednesday evening I was asked if I would like to take part in a military trophy competition, one that the troop had won several times in the past. To be honest I felt honoured to be asked, as those in charge obviously thought I had what it takes to be a part of a winning team. I accepted the offer, and it wasn't long before I, and the rest of the troop, were off to participate in the Military Skills Competition in Pirbright.

Chapter 5

Lambs to the Slaughter

Pirbright Barracks is much like all British army camps; a collection of bland accommodation blocks, and old wooden structures painted in an olive green drab. I believe the place has been updated now, however when I visited for the military skills competition I found it unimaginably depressing. Even more so when we were shown to where we would be sleeping for our 2 nights stay.

We arrived in the back of a 4 ton army truck, and were greeted at the gates by a couple of angry military police personnel who guided us over to the far side of the base. They simply pointed towards an old rundown wooden hut, and told us that would be where we were staying. It resembled one of the shacks from the television series Tenko. There were planks missing from the sides, it had a hole in the roof at one end, and the only good pieces of wood on the whole structure were the ones used to board up the broken windows it had.

Inside was even less inspiring. Steel sprung beds lined the room, and mattresses that were thinner than a slice of bread lay upon them. Ancient rusted lockers were up against the walls separating the bed spaces, and a pile of scaffold poles had been discarded in the main aisle.

As soon as I saw the room I instantly opted to kip in my sleeping bag outside that night. Anyway we were not there on holiday, we were there to try to win the Lamb Trophy.

The RLC (Royal Logistic Corps) Military Skills Competition is run every November and is open to both the regular army, and the TA's Major and Minor units. The regular army units compete for the Gore Trophy, whilst the Territorial units compete for the Lamb Trophy. The competition consists of an assault course, followed by a march and shoot. The rest of the event is a navigational exercise around Pirbright training area. In 2001 my commando unit had won the competition outright beating both the Regular and TA participants. So I felt slightly under pressure, and I hoped I wouldn't let the troop down. This worry became unfounded when later that day I saw the other TA units in the competition.

To be completely honest when I saw what we were up against I knew straight away that we were going to win. This is not me being big headed, it's just that we were the only commando unit going for the Lamb Trophy, and none of the other TA units were trained up to our level of fitness. After all, this was a logistic corps competition, and although a high level of fitness is needed in all branches of the military, those in logistics don't need to train as hard physically as battle frontline personnel do.

Come the evening the lads in the troop were itching to leave camp and hit the beer. With the competition starting early the following morning, and me not knowing what was in store for me, there was no way in hell I was going to drink. So I stayed in camp at our not so luxurious accommodation, while they all went out to some local watering hole. I was tucked up in my sleeping bag on the grass around the back of our rundown shack, when I heard them all stagger back around midnight. I took a look in the door to see just what level of ruin they were in, and saw that several of the lads were charging at each other up and down the middle of the room, using the scaffold poles that had been left there like jousts. Then they started sword fighting with them. I left them to it and retired to my place on the grass outside. I tried to get some sleep, but it wasn't easy listening to the medieval battle commencing inside.

Despite the level of shenanigans the lads got up to the previous evening, they were yet again fresh as daisies the following morning. We dressed in full combats, and grabbed our tactical webbing (a system of pouches used to carry ammunition and equipment, that is attached on a belt around the waist and supported with straps over the shoulders), and we set off to the competition ground.

The first part of the competition was a blur of us going through several tents and being tested on everything from first aid to navigation. After this we were all lined up in our teams, facing the start and the first challenge: the assault course.

While most of the other teams in front of us contained 6 personnel from their respective units, ours contained only 5. This was because some of the troop members hadn't renewed

45

their APWT (Annual Personal Weapons Test), a test every soldier must undertake each year to prove their safety and competence with a firearm. As we would be firing on a range during the test, if a person hadn't passed the APWT they could not shoot and were not allowed to run the course.

We stood there in the queue to the start line watching the other teams take flight down the assault course, their members were climbing the vertical ladder walls, crawling under cargo nets, and scrambling over walls. All the while this was going on the sky became darker, to a point eventually that it felt like it was crushing us, and we all knew rain was imminent, however we didn't anticipate just how much rain was about to hit us.

Just as our team approached the start line a bolt of lightning split the sky in half, and an almighty rumble of thunder shook the heavens above. The "Go" command was shouted out from the side-lines and we all took off towards the first obstacle: a giant vertical steel ladder buried in the ground and reaching for the sky. To say I was reluctant to climb this thing in a thunderstorm was an understatement, but I threw my fears away and just attacked it head on. This obstacle requires you to climb up one side, step over the top, and descend the other side. The problem with that is there are multiple people on the ladder at once, and someone will be ascending one side as you come down the other, avoiding getting your fingers crushed and receiving a boot to your face while navigating it is hard work.

I had just stepped off this ladder when the rain started, however this was no mere shower, it was a complete deluge!

It rained so heavily that it was hard to see more than 10 feet in front of me, and the noise of it pounding on my helmet was like a machine gun going off in my head. I ran on, ploughing through the fast filling puddles, crawling under the cargo nets that were now awash with mud, and climbing ropes. I soon tired as the weight of the rain and the mud soaked into my combat clothing. In fact I was so drained when I reached the last obstacle, which was a large cement lined pit, reminiscent of an empty swimming pool, I had to ask two of my team members to literally throw me out of it.

I finished the assault course completely breathless, and I now had a 7 mile speed march in front of me with a range shoot at the 4 mile point. We grabbed our SA80 rifles which were being guarded while we ran the assault course, and set off on a marked route to the firing range. The rain still continued to pour down as the thunderstorm sparked and grumbled overhead. It was a truly miserable experience again.

The run to the shooting range felt like it took forever, and by the time we got there I was a shivering mess. As much as we were moving I could not produce enough heat to stay warm. The cold November rain was just draining me of energy. I was checking my rifle for firing when I was told I wouldn't be shooting. They select 3 members of the team at random for the shoot and I wasn't one of them. I felt overwhelming relief at this, because I wouldn't have been able to hit the side of a double decker bus from 10 meters away, as my hands were shaking so badly.

I had to wait in a holding area until my fellow team members came back from the range, I used this time doing press ups and other exercises to get some heat back in my freezing muscles. Then we set off again. The rain had stopped now, and the sun began to shine through. After the brief stop at the range, I began to feel good again. I was warming up nicely in the sun, and we were all progressing as a unit really well. We passed many of the other TA teams on the last leg to the finish line, then we saw a regular paras (paras - members of the Parachute Regiment) team gaining on us.

Now we all knew that our team was not in competition with this paras team, as they were a regular army unit going for the Gore Trophy, and we were a TA unit going for the Lamb Trophy, but that didn't stop the competitive side of our brains from kicking in. All of us as a team pushed ourselves, our webbing was still soaked through and our rifles were now heavy as lead in our arms, yet we gave it our all.

We kept the para team at bay for a good mile before they eventually caught up with us and passed us. They were much younger than we were and far more capable, they also appeared remarkably dry and mud free, something we couldn't get our heads around.

Not letting up, we kept our pace all the way to the finish line, where we had to hand over our equipment for weighing to show that we hadn't dumped any load along the way.

All of us were wobbling on our legs and totally exhausted. The OC came over and patted us all on our backs, congratulating us for our gallant efforts. Then I looked around and we were surrounded by all the other teams, from both regular and TA units. All of them looked shattered, and in differing levels of destruction.

There have been many times over the years that I have pushed myself to the limits, both mentally and physically with the military. Sometimes when I have done this I have found emotion kicks in, and a lump starts to form in my throat. This day was the first time that lump in my throat turned to tears in my eyes. Now the competition was over, all the teams started intermingling and congratulating each other. At that moment no one knew who had come first or last, all we cared about was that we had shared an experience together that had pushed us to our limits, and we had prevailed. Even one of the NCOs from the paras came over to us saying how we gave their team a run for their money. Here I was in my 30s still managing to give someone in their early 20s some competition. I felt great pride, not just in myself, but for everybody that ran that day in such atrocious weather conditions. At that moment every single person on that field was a winner.

Later that afternoon we were informed that our team had won the Lamb Trophy. We were marched into a jam packed sports hall, and each team member was presented with a medal. Needless to say I relented that night and decided to join the troop for one of their legendary piss ups. I believe I deserved it.

Me and my TA unit at the end of the Lamb Trophy competition.

Chapter 6

Green Lid

The elation of winning the Lamb Trophy kept my spirits high for several weeks afterwards, however much like going on holiday, or throwing a party, when the buzz of it fades away you begin to look for a new way to get that buzz back again. I needed a new challenge, and for me that challenge was the All Arms Commando Course.

There are many books and documentaries on the AACC, and they will go into the course in far more depth than what I will write in here. I am merely going to outline some of my experiences as I did the shortened TA version of it. I am sure both regular Royal Marines and commando reservists will pick holes in what I have to say, however everyone's experience of the course is different, and this is mine.

When I was eventually given a date for the AACC, I upped my already heavy training schedule to an insane level. Even the troop as a whole changed their ways to help those going for the course. The weekends of getting pissed and going on jollies away, turned into endless hours of intense training. From speed marches of many miles carrying full combat gear, to spending long hours on the beach doing sit ups, press ups, and log carries in the surf. Trying to fit this in around a full time job was almost impossible, and eventually something had to give.

Luckily for me the government makes it a legal requirement for companies to allow employees time off for Territorial Army training. This didn't go down too well with my boss, who threatened to dismiss me at one point. He almost had a heart attack when I presented him with a letter from the government stating that if he sacked me for going away with the TA he would find himself in court facing charges.

Things may have changed now, but at the time I had to spend 9 weekends away at Lympstone, doing build up training. Then spend a further 2 full weeks there doing the commando tests, to earn the coveted green beret.

The build-up weekends were like going back to basic training again. The problem was I was over 10 years older now and I didn't take too kindly to being shouted at again as if I were a new recruit.

I shut my brain down to this abuse, knowing it was intended to break me down and put me off the tasks in hand. On these weekends I was also given the outline of what the final test week would involve.

I was taught and tested on all the core military skills again while training for the AACC, including field craft, tactics, patrolling, defence, weapons, signals, map reading, navigation, first aid, health, hygiene and physical training. Then I had to learn the following commando skills: amphibious assault drills, cliff assault drills, helicopter drills and small unit tactics.

During these course weekends away I also had to pass various physical tests. These tests had to be undertaken wearing boots, trousers and smock, while carrying fighting order equipment and my rifle. I had to achieve a 30ft (9.1m) rope climb. Run the infamous bottom field assault course in under 5 minutes. Fireman's carry a colleague over 200m while also carrying his and my own equipment and weapon (combined weight 62lbs (28kgs)), in 90 seconds. Show that I could comfortably achieve a full regain, over a tank filled with water as protection from falling. The regain involves candidates doing a Tyrolean traverse using no technical climbing equipment, only using skill and strength to cross along a rope strung between two towers. The technique is to balance your torso on top of the rope whilst pushing across using an ankle from one leg hooked over the rope and using the other leg to balance. During the traverse, you are required to halt and hang by your hands from the rope. Then you have to "regain" the traverse position on top of the rope; it's a move that requires both technique and strength. We were also required to do a 12 mile (19km) load carry at night, as a formed body (a formed body is a group route-marching in rough rank and file with no specific pace or step length) carrying 69lbs (31kgs) marching order equipment and personal weapon, this had to be completed within 4 hours.

Although extremely tough, I managed to accomplish all of the above tests. Only the 30ft rope climb caused me a problem. I struggled with it at first, but I was not going to be beaten. I spent every spare moment I had scaling that rope with full equipment and rifle until I perfected the technique.

Eventually I found myself faced with the final commando tests. The first week was a test exercise I will not go into, as I wouldn't want to ruin the fun for any would be recruits reading this and going for the course. The second and final week involved physical tests being completed on consecutive days. These were hard, these were tough, and they hurt me – a lot!

First up was the endurance course. This is an individual test comprising a challenging 6 mile (9.65 km) course whilst carrying 21lbs (9.5kgs) fighting order equipment and rifle. The first two miles consists of undulating woodland terrain featuring obstacles such as tunnels, pipes, wading pools and an underwater culvert (which I absolutely hated). The last 4 miles (6.43 km) were an obstacle-free metalled road return run back to the commando training centre. Everyone is required to complete this in 73 minutes. Following this we were required to do a marksmanship test, where a candidate must hit 6 out of 10 shots at a target on a range 200 meters away. I completed the endurance course and hit 8 out of the 10 shots I fired, passing this first test day unscathed.

The following day we did a 9 mile (14 km) speed march, as a formed body. Yet again, we were to be in full fighting order and with our rifles. This march had to be completed in 90 minutes (at an average pace of 6 miles per hour). I suffered on this one. I was still aching from the previous day's exertions and the weather was crap too. I also took a tumble towards the end of this march. Although we were taught how to handle a fall while load carrying equipment by doing a forward roll. Actually achieving an elegant roll when you are not expecting to trip up is another matter. I did indeed try to do a forward roll when I fell, however I smashed my right shoulder into the ground hard, and badly grazed the back of my right hand. I still completed the march within the time limit, but I was worried about how bad I may had injured my shoulder.

After an evening of packing my shoulder with ice, followed by a breakfast of pain killers the following morning, I was on to the next test – The Tarzan assault course. On this test we all started on the commando slide (a zip line) at 1 minute intervals apart. We were then confronted with a number of high aerial apparatuses followed immediately by the bottom field assault course. It finished with a rope climb up a 30ft near-vertical wall. All this must be completed whilst carrying fighting order and personal weapon in 13 minutes.

I started this test expecting to fail. My shoulder hurt from the previous day's fall, and I found it hard to grip with my right hand due to it being swollen from the graze that covered the back of it. However the moment I stood at the commando slide I pushed all of that to one side and just went for it. I focused on nothing else but getting to the next obstacle. That whole test is a blur in my mind. All I remember going down the zip line is me swearing in determination and pain all the way until I reached the top of the rope wall at the end. I was totally and utterly spent at the end, and it was another one of those times when I found myself overcome with emotion just by completing it.

The only thing separating me from completing commando training now was the final test: the 30 miler. This is a tactical navigation endurance march to be completed by a syndicate whilst carrying personal load carrying equipment, weapon, spare clothing and rations. All candidates must achieve this in 8 hours.

The 30 miler is arguably the hardest challenge of all the commando tests, but as I have stated in previous chapters I am more suited to load carrying over long distance than fast paced runs. So I wasn't too worried about doing this test, until I started marching that is.

We all set off on this final march in the early hours of the morning to avoid the heat of the day, and I felt drained from my very first step. I may be good at long distance carrying, but that is when I am feeling fresh. This time however, I was riding on the back of multiple test days and already feeling fatigued. My legs were like jelly for the first few miles, and the terrain of Dartmoor with its muddy trails, grassy lumps, and hidden holes, made the going very tough. There was a point early on where I started to have doubts that I would even make it to the half way point.

As I pushed on and shut my mind down the time and distance slowly ebbed away, and I found myself feeling better again. Over the years leading up to this I had been on more marches than I could count, however this one felt different. Not a single unnecessary word was said during the whole time we were out there. The only sounds were that of our foot falls, our equipment moving around on us, and the wind blowing across the top of the moorland grass. Every trooper was in their own little world with only one thing on their minds – finishing this task and earning that Green Beret.

Towards the end of the march I started suffering again, my calves and shins were screaming for me to stop, but nothing short of having a broken leg would have stopped me at that point.

The moment I saw the end in sight at Shaugh Prior Bridge, I almost burst into tears, I held them back this time though and found a private moment alone later that day to let them out.

I had passed the commando course and earned the Green Beret. I received it in a very impromptu ceremony (I believe those that did the commando course with the Royal Marines got a more formal one than we reservists did). At that moment I felt amazing pride in what I had achieved. I had followed in the footsteps of so many others who had endured the hardship of the commando course and prevailed. It shall be a moment that will live with me for the rest of my life.

I must say however (and this is my own personal opinion and I do not wish to disrespect or offend other reservists), that those who did the full Royal Marines Commando course had a far harder time of it. They had to endure the soul destroying discipline every single day for endless weeks. Yes I had to train physically just as hard, and learn all the same skills as they did, but I didn't have to put up with the military bullshit that goes with living in camp. I personally feel they earned that beret far more than I did.

I returned to my TA unit and was greeted with huge congratulations by all but two individuals who now saw me as a bigger threat than ever. The OC was delighted that he had another trooper who now possessed a "green lid" and was no longer a "crap hat" (crap hat – the term given to anybody that doesn't wear a commando or paratrooper beret).

I was instantly treated differently by those higher up in the troop after this. All formalities apart from addressing those in charge by their rank were gone. I had become part of their brotherhood, and it felt amazing. I had come a long way since working in a factory in Coventry all those years ago. Here I was in my early 30s, part of an elite team, and at the pinnacle of my fitness, what more could I need?

I was about to find out in the coming weeks…………

Chapter 7

Pastures New

In the weeks following the AACC I found myself having a lot more time to myself, as I was no longer spending long hours training. Yes I still trained hard to keep up a high level of fitness, but it didn't require the dedication needed before.

Having this extra time I realised I did have something missing in my life – companionship. I have never been a party person and I would rather shovel shit than go to a nightclub, so meeting members of the fairer sex didn't arise very often. I was merely playing around on my phone one evening when I stumbled on a website where you could meet others. I wasn't looking for a relationship and was only keen to find someone I could go to the cinema with on occasion, so I put a brief profile on.

I received a few replies from some crazy and bizarre individuals, who I wouldn't have dreamed of meeting up with even with all my military training behind me. Then I had a message from someone who appeared half normal, so I arranged a rendezvous with her at a popular Plymouth restaurant that overlooks the waterfront.

Little did I know at the time this woman would entirely change the course of my life.

Her name was Claire and we hit it off straight away. She was very outgoing, and enjoyed outdoor activates such as horse riding, sailing, and hiking. It was fantastic to meet someone that shared my enthusiasm for the outdoors, and adventure.

After this first initial meeting we started to get together on a regular basis for long walks, she even introduced me to sailing. Although the first time she took me out in a Laser dingy she capsized it, sending the boat full turtle and catapulting us both into the sea. Nothing like being thrown in at the deep end – literally.

She also owned a large static caravan out on the coast. When I visited we would go for long strolls around the coast path, and take in the spectacular views. Although I had been living in Plymouth for several years at this point, I had never truly explored the coast paths around South Devon. Going on those walks made my heart sing. The coast path is a truly magical place. I love everything about it: the way it rises and falls majestically as it hugs the upper cliffs, the tranquillity of it, and the wildlife it is home to.

I was still going away with my troop every other weekend, however I was starting to resent it. As my relationship with Claire blossomed, my feelings towards the TA started to sour. I cherished my time with Claire, and growing tired of weekends away watching my fellow troopers get hammered in the evenings, and then running myself ragged in the days.

I was still having troubles with a couple of the other troopers too. Their behaviour towards me was getting worse and bordering on out right bullying. Now I may have put up with being bullied in my younger years, but there was no way in hell I was going to stand for it as an adult. They pushed me and pushed me until one day my toleration for it reached a peak and I snapped.

I was walking down a corridor in the TA centre when I passed one of my aggressors, yet again he said a sly comment and shouldered against me. I had been putting up with this sort of crap for weeks and this time it was the final straw. I pinned him up against the wall and punched him. He instantly went running off to the OC about it, luckily for me the OC knew that the attitude of the other trooper was appalling and he sided with me. This wasn't the end of the matter though, I continued to have several run-ins with this said individual.

All of this bad attitude and behaviour by the two other troopers made me resent every minute I was spending with the TA. It put me on edge, I found myself being constantly on alert while in camp or away on exercises. This constant alertness started to cause pent up aggression, and I went on to have another "scuffle" on a training exercise just outside Oakhampton training camp.

We were out doing a 12 mile speed march in full combat gear. The troop were all strung out over several miles, and everyone was going at their own pace. I was towards the front of this spread out group and just coming to the top of a hill. The day was hot and I was in a foul mood. I resented being there sweating my arse off when I could have been out enjoying the sea views with Claire. As I crested the hill there was a military Land Rover parked up with two occupants inside that I didn't know. They were in combat fatigues, but not showing any rank. As I marched past the passenger side the person inside shouted in my ear "Get a fucking move on will you!"

I just flipped. I punched him in the face through the open window. I then pulled the door open and dragged him out. We fell to the ground grappling and continued landing punches on each other. Eventually he ended up kneeling on my chest pinning me against my Bergen. All my anger that had been building up for weeks came flooding out at once.

The other occupant of the Land Rover jumped out and pulled us apart. Soon afterwards I found myself facing the OC about this incident. I wasn't let off as lightly this time. Although the OC agreed with me again that someone that was not a troop member had no right to shout at me in the way they had, I should have shown restraint. Not only that, but the person in question that I chose to fight with was an ex-SAS soldier turned civilian, and out there that day on his way to film a television series about the Special Forces.

I received a small fine for my indiscretion, however this incident sealed the deal with me and the troop. I was tired of feeling down and depressed with the TA, and just wanted the happiness and contentment I felt in my life outside of it, so I quit. I handed all my kit in 2 weeks later and left. I had an amazing experience with the unit, I met some fantastic friends, and will always cherish the memories I have of those early years with the troop, and completing the AACC. However it was time for me to move on to another adventure in life, and that was with Claire.

I continued doing training runs in my spare time, and even ran alongside Claire on a few occasions while she was out horse riding. Running which started to feel like a chore when I was doing it with the TA, wasn't anymore. I was doing it for me again, and it felt fantastic.

There was only one downside: I no longer had anything lined up to truly challenge me. I was glad to be free of the military, but I always liked pushing myself to see how far I could go and how much I could take.

So to challenge myself I started going longer distances, and then trying to beat my own times. However this still didn't quench my thirst for something harder to do.

One day Claire said she knew a person who had an entry to the Plymouth half marathon. They couldn't make the run due to other commitments and would I like to run in their place. Outside of the military I had never participated in any organised runs. Sure I had seen many on television, and even walked past a few, yet I had never entered any. I never saw large running events as being my sort of thing: being shoulder to shoulder with thousands of participants jostling for an inch of road over countless miles. But I have never been one to back down from a challenge and I accepted the place.

It was only 5 days between being asked if I would like to run the half marathon and the actual race start, so I didn't train for the race as such, I just ran it on the back of my normal training routine.

Although I was expecting a large gathering on race day, nothing prepared me for the mayhem that I found on Plymouth Hoe. The usually serene wide open tarmacked space that overlooks Plymouth Sound and the channel beyond, was overflowing with thousands of people dressed in a multitude of bright running gear. Large gazebos and trailers were lined up in rows, some selling food, others selling running products or advertising local services. Music, which was being blasted out from immense speakers, was intermittently broken by a voice doing random announcements. It was chaos!

I shuffled around in this random sea of craziness for half an hour before the crowd started to line up between barriers that funnelled towards the start line. Being a complete virgin to this type of event, I found the experience very claustrophobic. I felt like vaulting the barriers and running to the very back of the running pack just to get some elbow room. Luckily it wasn't long before we got underway.

When the signal to start went off, nothing seemed to happen. I looked above the heads of those in front of me and saw a ripple of movement draw towards me from the start line. Bobbing and moving heads slowly drew closer indicating that those runners had set off. The wave eventually hit my segment, and we began shuffling forward.

The first 2 miles were a very uncomfortable experience for me. I found it almost impossible to find any space, and I was concentrating more on trying not to trip up over other competitors than actually running. Everyone appeared to be running at differing paces. I'd have runners in front of me going painfully slow, and have others behind me trying to overtake. On top of this there were many obstacles along the streets I had to try to navigate around, such as road signs, bollards, and parked cars.

Eventually as we approached Saltram Country Park, the road got wider and I found some breathing room. Those that had started off too quickly began to slow and I found myself over taking many other runners. The frustration I felt at the start faded away and I began to truly enjoy myself. I had never ran through crowds of cheering spectators before and it was a brilliant experience. Seeing so many people clapping and encouraging all of us runners along made the whole running experience easier, every time I passed a cheering crowd it felt like I was running on a cushion of air with the wind on my back, and the miles just passed by without effort.

Before I knew it I was running through Plymouth Barbican, and heading back towards the Hoe and the finish line. I found myself sprinting the last 100 hundred meters to the finish line, to the sound of roaring crowds. It was amazing.

I received my medal and moved along into the finishing area which was a large gazebo with an assortment of various foods on large tables. I grabbed a chicken pasty and a bottle of water and set off in search of Claire amongst the still heaving mass of people.

I was sat in the passenger seat of Claire's car as she drove me home, gazing down proudly at the finishers' medal I now had hanging around my neck. Then I looked up to see that we were passing a part of the course that still had runners going around it. I had run the half marathon in 1 hour 37 minutes, a far from impressive time. I had also finished the race some half an hour before we started driving back home, yet there were still several participants shuffling around at this 8 mile point of the course, with a further 5 miles to go.

I instantly felt huge admiration for them. They were still out there persevering, and would continue to be long after I had got home and started relaxing. So many people talk only about those that win races or are competitive, but few speak of the back of the pack runners who keep going long after the front runners have finished. For me they deserve just as much respect, if not more. Not just because of the physical effort involved, but the mental effort it takes to push on and not give up long after the cheering crowds have dispersed.

I enjoyed the Plymouth half marathon so much that I found myself itching for more races. Within a week I had sent off entries to several more. I completed the Exeter half marathon, Torbay half marathon, and countless 10k races all within the year. My Plymouth half marathon medal which at first hung by itself from my study curtain rail, fast got joined by many others, which eventually threatened to pull the whole thing off of the wall. Claire joined me on races too completing several 10k's.

My relationship with Claire continued to blossom and in July of 2008 I asked her to marry me on a gondola in Venice. We had backpacked the length of Italy, from Sorrento in the south, through Rome, up to Venice in the north. We experienced poverty, hardship, and elation on our journey, and I realised I would never want anyone else by my side in such situations but Claire. I wanted to spend the rest of my life with her, and proposing was a truly magical moment.

I was the happiest I had been in years, and I felt contented again challenge wise, I was out doing official races most weekends and didn't think I needed any more than that. Yet again I was proven wrong, when one day I had a chance meeting with an old forces friend.

My friend Patrick who was now out of the military and doing close protection work abroad, was visiting family in Plymouth and asked to meet up. We had a leisurely daytime drink on the Barbican overlooking the harbour and talked about old times. Then he asked me what I was currently doing. I went over my work and home life, and casually mentioned that I ran half marathons and other various races at weekends. He suggested to me that I should read a book called Survival of the Fittest by Dr Mike Stroud, the famous Arctic and Antarctic explorer who accompanied Sir Ranuplh Fiennes on many expeditions, including the first unsupported crossing of the Antarctic continent.

After our brief get together I went home and ordered a copy of the book he suggested online. This book changed my view of running and endurance entirely, and sent me down a path I never thought possible. It introduced me to a concept and distance of running I had never heard of before – the ultra marathon.

Chapter 8

Marathon and Beyond

In his fascinating book based soundly in medical science, Mike Stroud describes how we as humans evolved in a way that gave us an endurance advantage over other animals. When we were still hunter gatherers on the planes of Africa several thousands of years ago, we used to hunt in packs to bring in food for our communities. Early humans may have developed the ability to fashion tools and hunting weapons, however they are useless if you cannot get up close to prey. Antelope and other four legged mammals would simply take flight and outpace us, literally leaving us in their dust. Being our top speed is restricted due to us being bipedal (two legged), we developed endurance instead. Early humans were slow (indeed we still are) however we can go on at that slow pace unabated for many hours and even days. Our hunter gatherer ancestors simply ran their faster paced prey to the point of exhaustion, then brought them down with their weapons.

This athletic endurance is still with us today, it is bred into each and every one of us, however we no longer tap into it, because we now go to the supermarket for our food, we don't hunt it.

In his book Dr Stroud, who is still a practicing hospital physician, and former advisor to the Ministry of Defence, analyses individual feats of survival and endurance. He dissects his own challenging experiences of crossing Antarctica with Ranulph Fiennes, running the famous Marathon des Sables in the Sahara, and participating in gruelling cross-country endurance races in the United States. He also tells stories of other individuals whose feats of endurance are nothing short of remarkable.

When I finished his book, I was hungry for more. I instantly hit the internet looking up more books on the subject of extreme endurance. The first book I stumbled upon was Ultramarathon Man: Confessions of an All-Night Runner by Dean Karnazes. This was another book that absolutely blew me away.

Although he was an American high school runner, Dean Karnazes never achieved much athletic wise in his early years. On his 30th birthday however he experienced a bit of a conscience crisis that led to him leaving a party and spontaneously going out and running 30 miles. It laid him flat for several days afterwards, but the experience changed him as a person, and he went on to achieve some absolutely astonishing feats of endurance.

Since his 30th birthday running epiphany, Dean has ran 350 miles in 80 hours 44 minutes without sleep. Completed "The Relay", a 199 mile run from Calistoga to Santa Cruz, eleven times. Ran a marathon to the South Pole in -25 Celsius temperatures without snowshoes. Ran a marathon in each of the 50 US states in 50 consecutive days. He has won the 135 mile Badwater Ultramarathon across Death Valley, in 49 Celsius (120 F) temperatures, and had 5 other top 10 finishes in it too. He has ran 3000 miles across the United States from Disneyland to New York City, in 75 days, running 40 to 50 miles per day. He has also ran 148 miles in 24 hours on a treadmill. These are only a few of his achievements, and he still adds to this list all the time, and he is currently 59 years of age as I write this.

The list of endurance milestones that Dean Karnazes has accomplished appear impossible when first read, however he is far from alone in accomplishing such feats. There are hundreds if not thousands of people out there that have participated in events like these and excelled.

The more I researched the world of ultramarathons the more I realised it wasn't just the odd person that had freaky abilities to go beyond endurance, it was a whole community of individuals who sought out just how far they could push themselves. I learned that you didn't have to come from an athletic background, or have parents that were Olympic gold medallists. You just had to have two things to achieve these goals: a good training programme, and more importantly, an iron-willed determination when faced with overwhelming hardship.

My brother Sean, to whom I had mentioned a new found interest in ultramarathons, gave me a book on my birthday titled – Running Through the Wall: Personal Encounters with the Ultramarathon. It is a truly fascinating and gripping compilation of stories written by individuals who have ran ultramarathons all over the world. This book was the final straw that tipped the balance, I was determined to try to run ultra-distance. Yes I had achieved a distance beyond 26.2 miles of a marathon before, when I completed the endurance test on the commando course. But I had not ran it as a personal challenge. Plus all these books I had read left me with a question – Just how far could I go if I really tried?

Well I was about to find out. I went straight onto the internet and started researching ultra marathons in the UK, and to my surprise I found countless events all over, from the highlands of Scotland, to Lands' End in Cornwall. I didn't realise until then just how prolific ultra-distance races were, it made me wonder why I hadn't heard about them before.

As I scanned through the many events from 100 mile trail races up in the Yorkshire Dales, to 50 mile ones down in Kent, I stumbled on an ultra that was right on my doorstep here in Plymouth. It is called the Dartmoor Discovery, or DD as it is affectionately known. It is 32 miles in distance and is the UK's longest single lap road ultra marathon, starting and finishing in Princetown out on Dartmoor.

As I read through several reviews of the race, all of which highlighted the fact that the route was notoriously hilly, I thought of it as the perfect distance to start out exploring this world of ultra-running. After all 32 miles is only a marathon followed by a 10k. The problem was I hadn't even run an official marathon at that point, so I was basing that thought on the fact that so many people with minimum athletic background participated in events such as the London Marathon. Surely if anybody can train for a marathon, I could add on the 10k afterwards with a bit of extra effort.

I printed off the entry form and details, and read that to qualify for the race I needed to complete an official marathon in under 4 and half hours, within a year of the start date. It was late March 2009, and the DD race start was on 7th of June. Not wanting to wait until the following year to go for this ultra, I went back online and looked up official Marathons in the South West. At the top of the list of upcoming events was the Taunton Marathon, being held on 5th of April, less than 2 weeks away.

I asked myself, "Am I trained enough to do the 26.2 miles of a marathon?" Well I was going to find out. I filled out the entry form and sent it off. Many times over the years I have questioned myself about being ready for certain events, and I have always just shut my brain down to those thoughts and said the words in my head – "I'll deal with it on the day!" If you think too much about such things you will talk yourself out of doing them before you even begin, then regret afterwards not knowing if you could have actually achieved it.

I posted the entry form and felt excited again. An adventure was just around the corner; a marathon in less than 2 weeks' time, and an ultra in little over 2 months if I completed the marathon in the allotted time. I went out and treated myself to a long run. The sun blazed down from a clear spring sky and bathed me in its warmth - I was in my element. Little did I know that in 2 weeks' time the spring warmth would be replaced with frigid cold temperatures.

On the morning of the Taunton Marathon race I found myself scraping ice off Claire's car as she told me the temperature on the dashboard was reading 3 degrees C. There was a strong wind too, and it felt mind numbingly cold. As we left Devon and reached the M5 motorway, snow started to fall. I was sat in the passenger seat in shorts and t-shirt, questioning my sanity of running in such conditions. I had trained in far worse weather before, however I was usually equipped in appropriate military gear for it, not running attire.

We arrived in Taunton and it wasn't any warmer. It was clear of snow, but the biting cold was penetrating. We stayed in the car until as close to the start time as possible in a bid to stay warm. Then 5 minutes before the start, I shuffled off to the start line and Claire joined the many spectators lining the route.

Standing amongst the other runners I was surrounded by an orchestra of chattering teeth and shaking bodies. Everyone was desperately waiting for the signal to start. Each minute felt like an eternity, and a small group of us started chatting about where we had travelled from, yet we all sounded drunk as we slurred our words through quivering lips.

Eventually we were set off and it was a relief to just be moving. It took me the first 2 miles to warm up, however those miles were through the town centre and the cheering crowds helped take my mind off of the cold.

The Taunton marathon is actually a 13 mile 2 lap loop out from the town centre, and through country lanes. Runners can opt to do 1 lap if they wish to go for a half marathon, or 2 (like I was) for the full marathon distance. This meant that many of the other competitors disappeared early on, as they were doing the half marathon and going at a faster pace.

I leisurely plodded along and eventually got into my running grove. The miles ticked by and I started to enjoy being out there in the crisp air, gazing at the rolling hills of the countryside. I felt so fresh physically at the 11 mile point that I decided to pick up the pace slightly just to make sure I got in a good time to qualify for the Dartmoor Discovery.

I got running alongside 2 other guys who were doing the half marathon, one of which was attempting his first. They thought I was crazy for going around twice. When I explained I was doing it just so I could qualify for an even longer race in a couple of months' time, they looked at me like I needed certifying.

We approached the start/finish line where the half marathon runners would finish and I would begin my second lap. The cheering crowds lining the area lifted my spirits again, and as I bid farewell to those whose race was ending, I ploughed on at my increased pace.

There were not many doing the full marathon, and on lap 2 I got a few strange looks as pedestrians, who didn't see the earlier race start or were even aware of it, wondered why a guy on his own was running down the high street with a number on his front.

I soon left the town centre behind me and was back out on the country lanes. It was a welcome relief to be back out there and away from the traffic, however I started to feel slightly drained. I slowed my pace again, but I was losing energy fast. My head started spinning in dizziness and my legs became jelly like. I knew what it was but tried to push through it. I had read about it many times and felt it a few times myself on training exercises, I had hit – the wall!

As we run we burn up glycogen which is stored in our liver and muscles, it is our primary source of (stored) energy. When we run out of glycogen our body then starts using fat and protein as its fuel, however there is a price to pay as it switches over to doing that – you hit "the wall" and feel absolutely crap!

For many it happens at around the 20 mile point in a race, or 2 hours of intense exercise, and it varies in severity between individuals. For me it happened at the 17 mile point and I was suffering big time. I stopped running and pushed on at a fast walking stagger, I knew there was a drinks station just up the road that I passed on the first lap and decided I'd walk to it and try to recover there.

The drinks station was a large foldable picnic table with empty cups on and two large jugs of water. When I passed it on my previous lap there were a whole group of boy scouts handing out drinks, this time however there was a single scout standing behind the table with no one else in sight. I stumbled up to the table and the young lad who was maybe 11 years old asked me if I would like a drink. I nodded my head and said "Yes please." He then picked up a full cup of water and threw it over me, soaking me from my face down to my waist. He then ran off laughing. The water was freezing cold and I was stood there in complete and utter shock. I was feeling awful before he did it and now I felt completely demoralised.

I think back at this incident now and laugh, but at the time I thought "You little bastard, I'd run after you if I had the energy and throw you in a river!"

I turned away from the drinks station and carried on down the road in my sodden state. I tried to get back into a steady jog to get some heat back into my system after the soaking, but I was still too drained of energy. I pushed on at a fast walk, it was only after another mile that my body started to sort itself out and I was able to run again.

The last 3 miles of the race were a blur, I just wanted it over with, and I was oh so glad to see the finish line. There were no crowds this time, just the odd person, and my wonderfully dedicated fiancée Claire to congratulate me. Seeing her at the end was like the sun coming out on a rainy day.

Unlike many of the other half marathons and events I had done previously, there were no food stalls or warm drink stands at the finish line, but a water dispenser, which contained ice cold water. I was desperate for something warm to eat and drink, but I pushed that out of my head at that moment. The most important thing was I had ran the marathon in 3 hours 55 minutes, a far from brilliant time, but one that would qualify me for the DD. It had been a hard race, especially the second lap, but I had achieved my goal. I could now attempt my first ultra marathon, plus it was going to be in June, at least it'd be warmer then, right? Wrong!!!

Chapter 9

Dartmoor Discovery

After returning from the Taunton marathon I asked myself "Could I have ran another 10k after the finish line?" After all, that's how much further I would have to go in the Dartmoor Discovery, plus the Taunton marathon was a very flat course. This ultra marathon, however, was notoriously hilly. Yet again, I pushed those thoughts out of my mind and told myself I'd deal with whatever I encountered on the day.

My legs were stiff for several days after the marathon and it took me a week before I got back fully into training again. I spent a lot of time reading up on what other ultra-runners did to build up to races, their training and their diets. Some runner's lives literally revolved around the races they were doing. Their whole way of life was structured to winning. To me though these races were a mere personal challenge, and there was only so much sacrifice I was willing to make for them, after all my goal was to merely complete them, not win.

Ultimately I ignored all that I read diet wise and just carried on eating my normal food. I also ignored the advice that you should tapper off your running towards race day (i.e. do shorter distances to let your body recover). Tapering training was not a concept we were ever privileged with in the forces.

If anything I was trained to do consecutively longer runs every day, culminating in the longest one being on the last day of training. So I carried on doing 5 to 10 mile runs a few days a week, which are quite short distances in the world of ultra race training.

In the weeks building up to the DD event the weather improved and I was slightly concerned about just how hot I may be out on Dartmoor running in the blazing June sunshine for hours on end. This was an unfounded worry however, as the day before race day the weather turned and cold temperatures and rain were predicted for the high moors.

Claire who was now expecting our first child stayed at home for this race and her dad Alan volunteered to support me on race day. As Alan and I left Plymouth and drove out towards Dartmoor the temperatures plummeted and the sky became dark and gloomy. When we arrived at Princetown the temperature was a very unseasonable 5 degrees C, far from the June heat I was worrying about in the build up to the race.

Being we had arrived so early Alan suggested we should drive the first few miles of the route so I could see what lay instore for me in the early stages of the race, which I thought was a fantastic idea. So we drove out past the picturesque Two Bridges Hotel and along the B3357 towards Dartmeet. We ventured out for the first 5 miles of the course, and apart from a very slight hill it was largely flat. Little did I know that this small section that we recced was the only flat part of the whole course.

Alan spun the car around and we headed back to Princetown, the sky was growing darker by the minute and it threatened to rain. We pulled into a carpark at the back of the Plume of Feathers pub and I started to prepare for the race. As I pinned my number on my t-shirt just before race start, Alan offered me a long sleeve running top to put on over the running t-shirt I was wearing as the temperature was so cold. I do believe if he hadn't given me that extra layer the outcome of my race on the day would have been completely different.

As race time approached a gathering of runners of all varieties and ages assembled in the road in the middle of Princetown. It was very chilly, yet everyone was in high spirits. Runners were spreading "good lucks" and handshakes to friends and strangers alike.

"BANG!!!!!" I was largely unprepared for the race start signal which was a firework rocket. The whole crowd flinched then set off at a jog down the road to Two Bridges. Right from the start the wind was in my face, however I started to warm up and the first 6 miles were wonderful, nice scenery, and as I knew from the earlier drive, generally flat. This changed dramatically when we all got to Dartmeet.

I arrived at Dartmeet to cheering crowds who lined a small bridge. I was then confronted by a hill of biblical proportions! It was a near vertical climb which cars are forced to take in first gear. There was a snake of runners spread out on it all walking. I knew this was still very early in the race so took a steady stroll up it. The climb was so steep though that even walking was very tough. The one consolation in races like these is you are surrounded by so many others who are going through the same experience and pains. Just as I crested the top it started to drizzle. Within minutes that drizzle progressed to ice cold rain. The rain became so heavy I found it hard to see through it, luckily we were running on roads with marshals who were directing us, otherwise I'd have gotten easily lost.

The next few miles were a series of undulating hills, some shin breaking descents through Poundsgate and Newbridge, then on to Ashburton, which is at the 13.5 mile point. I knew from reading about the race that there is a 1.3 mile hill climb out the back of Ashburton. You can read about these things all you like but nothing can truly prepare you for them. This climb was an absolute killer and cannot be truly described without profanity. That hill felt like it went on forever, and just when I thought I had reached the top, I went around a bend in the road and it climbed again into the far distance, it was soul destroying. When I finally reached the top I felt like planting a flag in the summit.

The rain continued to pour down relentlessly and I started suffering badly. Although I was running, I couldn't produce enough heat to stay warm and I was shivering badly. I also couldn't open and close my hands fully. As I stopped at a drinks station which was under a gazebo, I tried to pick up some Jelly babies from a bowl on a table. Try as I may I couldn't grip them, they just kept tumbling out of my cupped hands, and I had to embarrassingly ask one of the marshals to put them in my mouth.

I continued on in the downpour and got into "the mode." When in this state of mind I shut myself off to everything around me and try to concentrate on one thing alone. I find targets to aim for further down the road and just head for them, be they lamp posts, curves in the road, or junctions, I make them my whole point of focus and think of nothing else, that way I break the race down into smaller more manageable steps in my mind. Another thing I do when suffering or struggling on long training runs (something I adopted early on in my military training) is counting; I will count in my head up to 100 and back down to zero. I find it helps take my mind off of the pain I'm going through.

Yet again the next few miles became a blur, however I still remember encountering clapping marshals, and people standing road side with food and drinks. It was so wonderful to see so many dedicated people supporting us all in such atrocious conditions, and I wish I could go back and thank them all individually.

I encountered Alan several times along the way too as he drove around the course following my progress, and my deterioration. He must have wondered just what sort of lunatic his daughter was going to marry.

I pressed on and it got tougher, and tougher. Several big hills and insane descents wore me down as I watched the miles slowly tick by....18, 22, 24.... As I approached marathon point on the high moors I just wanted someone to put me out of my misery. The savage wind was blasting the freezing rain horizontally into me and I was plodding along in an absolute daze. I carried on, thinking "It's only a 10k now, you can do this, 6 miles more and you can have a warm drink." But as much as I tried to convince myself, I knew I was in a bad way and may not make it to the finish line.

Shortly after marathon point I went around a left hand bend and found myself on the B3212 that headed back towards Two Bridges, and Princetown. I was relieved that I was heading back towards the finish, but I was starting to come unglued. I could no longer count in my head, I was finding it hard to concentrate and focus, and my shivering was approaching uncontrollable levels, so much so that I was afraid of shaking my fillings out of my teeth.

I saw the second to last water station of the course in the distance and thought to myself "What am I doing?" These words rang in my head like church bells as I tried frantically to plant my next step, the road was flowing with water like a mountain stream from the torrential downpour around me. I was freezing. I wasn't prepared for this. And I knew I was in trouble.

A thousand and one thoughts rushed through my head as I tried to comprehend the situation I found myself in, "Come on you can do this, you're 29 miles in, only 3 to go. Do I have 3 miles left in me?"

"Yes. No. Yes...... So cold.... must concentrate... focus.... so cold."

I was losing it, and when I finally stopped shivering, I knew I was experiencing the early stages of hypothermia, but I continued on regardless. I found myself at the water station a gibbering mess, sponges that were intended to cool competitors as we sweltered in the expected June heat, I used to wipe the 5 degree rain from my face with. One of the marshals asked me my name, I couldn't answer. I felt lost inside. My head was spinning, "What is my name?"

Then another runner came into the drinks station behind me. Rain continued to pour down around us. It was as cold as ice and as hard as nails. The runner was a female at about 25 years of age. She staggered in, hunched over, and then became violently sick. Marshals rushed to her aid. I fell to my knees in a puddle, as I looked up there was an old man under an umbrella, he was glancing over at the runner that had just collapsed and said, "Now there is a young lady who has given it her all." I turned back and saw her being tended to. Then I looked down the road ahead, knowing I had not yet given my all. Not just yet. I still had energy left in me. I got up and started moving again.

Only stubbornness got me through the last 3 miles of the race, because it certainly wasn't athletic ability or common-sense. When I saw Two Bridges Hotel and knew Princetown was a short distance away, I bellowed a huge "Yes!" to the heavens above. I may have been in a sorry state, but the last few hundred meters of the race were a very emotional experience. The cheering spectators made me feel like a winner no matter what position I was finishing in. The rain, which had been relentless for so long, only subsided as I crossed the finish line.

Alan was there to greet me, and so were several marshals who gave me a blanket and a warm cup of tea. The finish area was bustling with activity. There were runners wrapped in blankets and sat in chairs, supporters and spectators were weaving in and out, but it was an incredible atmosphere.

As I began to warm up Alan dialled up Claire on his mobile phone and handed it to me. It took everything in my power not to burst into tears when I heard her voice on the other end. She congratulated me on finishing my first ultra marathon, however I could never have done it without her, for she, and the wonderful new life she now had growing in her tummy, were in my heart and my head every single step of the way around.

On the drive back home I was sat in the passenger seat feeling completely drained, and I vowed to myself that I would never do a race like that again. A couple of days later the official finisher times from the day were put on line and I was amazed to see that I had gotten around the course in 5 hours 19 minutes, I was also middle of the field, far ahead of many other runners. This gave me a massive confidence boost. As the days ticked by and the post-race aches faded away from my muscles, I went back on my previous vow not to do the race again, and I decided I would indeed enter it again the following year.

I like many other runners, swear we will never go back and do certain races or distances again when the pain of them is still fresh in our minds, however as time goes by we forget about the misery we experienced on race day, we end up only thinking of the good parts and the elation of finishing. I believe we as humans have evolved this trait to get us through harsh times, and let's be honest, if we didn't have the ability to forget about suffering would women go back and have a second child after the pain of the first?

In the months following the DD I continued on competing in 10k's and half marathons, plus various other races, but they no longer had the same feel to them as before, and they now failed to challenge me. If anything I started disliking running in crowds and on streets. I craved trail running and the splendour of nature, not the urban jungles of the city races. I found myself looking for more ultra distance races, but they would have to wait, as a new adventure was about to begin: I was going to become a father.

In October of that year (2009) Claire gave birth to our first child Logan. She experienced a difficult labour, and Logan had to be ventilated due to inhaling meconium during birth. He was in NICU for observation for the first 24 hours of his young life, however he recovered quickly and was otherwise a healthy baby boy. It is very difficult to express in words alone the feeling of bringing another life into this world with someone you love. I felt completely overwhelmed with emotion, and when I saw Claire holding Logan in her arms in the hospital bed, I knew that no matter what races, goals, or other achievements I would go on to have in my life, it would never beat that moment.

Elizabeth Stone once said "Making the decision to have a child is momentous. It is to decide forever to have your heart go walking around outside your body." That is so very true, taking care of, and nurturing something as precious as another human life is a massive responsibility. It brings out the best and worst in all of us, but it can inspire you too. The moment Claire and I became parents, and we started our own little family, my inspiration and passion soared. I felt a new power in me too, a strength I never had before, and it was one I would find myself using in my future races.

Chapter 10

Finding the Limits

Shortly after giving birth to our son Logan, Claire got back into running again, and 7 months later in May of 2010 she ran the Plymouth Half Marathon crossing the line with her dad Alan. Her determination to get back into running so soon after giving birth and while still breast feeding, was inspirational to witness.

In September of that year Claire and I got married, it was a truly magical day and we were blessed with amazing weather. In my life I have never been through so much, and endured so much with another. We have experienced loss and triumph, endured hardship, and felt luxury. We have travelled tens of thousands of miles together, and seen what amazing things this planet has to offer. If I had to walk through the worst hell ever, I would never choose anyone but her to be beside me, and if I saw her in danger I would lay my life down for her in an instant. She is my soul mate and I can never thank her enough for all she has given me. She is the only person who truly knows and understands me, and marrying Claire truly completed me.

I continued doing more running events, and I returned to do the Dartmoor Discovery again the following year as I had planned.

Claire and her dad Alan finishing the Plymouth half marathon.

It was a completely different experience than the first time. The weather was hot and I suffered in the heat, but it was nowhere near as painful as before. Claire supported me around the route this time while her parents cared for Logan. It took me longer than the previous year, and I finished in 5 hours 45 minutes, mostly because I went extremely slow towards the end and just enjoyed the scenery of Dartmoor.

I pressed on doing more events, the Grizzly over in Dorset, and various other trail races. I went back again and did the Dartmoor Discovery in 2011, then entered a 44 mile race around the coast of Cornwall, from Lizards Point to Lands' End, called the Classic Quarter. It was a race I thoroughly enjoyed. As usual it had its pains. I got lost at one point even though we were following the coastline and all I had to do was keep the sea to my left. The climbing towards the end of the race was hair raising to say the least.

However I loved being out there not just racing but enjoying nature, there were sections of the course where I didn't see anyone for miles and I loved that.

I still hadn't found my limit though - the point where I could go no further. I even started to do training runs exceeding 30 miles just to see if I could spontaneously go beyond marathon distance any time I wanted to. Many of my friends thought I was crazy going that distance and not getting anything for it such as a trophy or a medal. It was impossible to explain to them that the only reward I was seeking, was to see if I could complete the distance, and to prove to myself I had it in me to do so.

On the hottest July day of 2012, Claire gave birth to our second son Owen, and our family was complete. Owen's birth unlike Logan's was uncomplicated. He came into this world glowing red, and the first thing his little ears heard were the sound of me crying at the joy of being a father again. Tears flowed from my eyes like Niagara Falls as I cradled him in my arms.

Everybody who raises children and tries to continue a hobby or pastime such as running, knows it is a fine balancing act, of course your children take priority, they always will, but at any given opportunity you bolt for the door to get a training run in. On my shorter routes I could take the children out in a pushchair, however on longer runs, especially where trails were involved, it was logistically impossible. Claire, supportive as ever encouraged me to continue my pursuits, and when I said I was interested in entering a 100 mile event the following year, she just waved her hand and said "Go for it."

The event I was looking at was called the Ultra Trail South West (UTSW). It was actually 104 miles in length and participants had 36 hours in which to complete it. Race start was to be at a place called Polruan on the south coast of Cornwall, competitors would follow the coast path east to Looe, then head north and traverse Bodmin Moor, join the north Cornish coast at Boscastle and follow the coast path there west to Newquay. The course was extremely hilly with

21,000 feet of ascent along the way, however that just added to the challenge for me.

Like always I put my entry in with little thought and declared to deal with the distance on race day. I must say though I did train harder for this event than others I had done up to that point. I knew with a distance like the one involved I couldn't just wing it, even top seasoned ultra marathoners DNF(Do Not Finish) races of that distance, after all an awful lot can happen in 104 miles and 36 hours.

I changed my training runs, and instead of concentrating on my distance I focused on how many hours I could keep going for. At first I'd do 2 hour training runs, then 4, then 6. There eventually reaches a point though where you can go out for only so many hours with a young family at home. Also logistically it's not easy to go for 6 hours straight and carry everything you need, unless you do laps that pass somewhere you can replenish your water supplies. Fitting that level of training in around 8 hour working days too became very tough.

Yet again I put in an entry for the Dartmoor Discovery; it was my fourth year of entering the race and it was being held only 3 weeks before the start of the UTSW. Little did I realise when I first ran the DD and suffered in the freezing rain, that I would eventually use the race in the future as a training platform for bigger things.

Before I knew it UTSW race day was upon me. The day started off as an endurance event in itself. I was up at 4:30am with the children after a restless night, and I had to complete a few work related jobs before Claire could drive me to the Watergate Bay Hotel near Newquay for the 1pm race check in.

When Claire dropped me off at midday I already felt tired, however I thought I would get a chance to rest before the 6pm start time. I bid her farewell and entered the hotel. Inside it was a bustling sea of bodies; it reminded me of frantic stock exchange scenes regularly broadcast on news bulletins. It was rammed with runners and guests all moving around in a frenzy. It took 3 hours to go through kit checks, hand my drop bag in (which had extra clothes and food in that would be transported to certain checkpoints along the way), and go through the race briefing. The waiting around drained my mental energy. When everyone finally got through the kit checks we were all ushered outside to get on a bus, which was to transport us to the race start on the south coast. The bus, which was due at 4:30pm, finally arrived at 6:15pm after breaking down twice. This waiting period was harsh on all of us. We were just desperate to start the race.

The bus journey was one of pure terror as the driver bombed down country lanes like he was in a rally. I gripped on to the side of my seat and feared for my life as the lunatic driver, who had obviously seen the Keanu Reeves film Speed, tried to keep the bus over 50 miles per hour even on the sharpest of corners. When we finally stopped in a carpark I couldn't get off the bus fast enough, however the journey did clear the earlier tired feelings from my mind.

We were all led from the carpark out through a kissing gate and into a field overlooking the sea. I was surrounded by a total of 74 other runners of all shapes, sizes, races and appearances. I love the feeling before a race, it gives me a buzz being present amongst so many individuals who share the same goal as me, and in this case it was to run, walk or crawl 104 miles to a distant finish line in under 36 hours.

A man with a megaphone appeared and gave us all another brief outline of what lay ahead, then wished us good luck. So on Friday 21st June 2013, at 7:30pm (some 1 and half hours later than the arranged race start time), I found myself in Polruan, South Cornwall at the start of my longest race event so far. Megaphone man started the count down. We all joined in in a booming chorus that echoed off the cliffs "3.....2.....1.... AAARRRGGHHH!!!!"

Leg 1: Polruan to Looe, 11.8 miles, 2,260feet of climbing.

We all started off at a fair pace. The coastal path in this area was very narrow so we were all forced into single file. Right from the start, I was pushed into a pace well beyond what I wanted to be in. I tried to let those faster than me past but passing places were few.

Over the days leading up to the race weather reports for the weekend were bad: a band of wind and heavy rain was expected over night, but none of us expected scorching sunshine in the hours leading up to it.

Although it was approaching 8pm and we had a coastal breeze, the sun was blazing down on us hard. After about 3 miles the path widened, allowing us all to find our own pace, I found myself in a group of 6 chatty blokes. One guy was from California over here on a working holiday and living the adrenaline life, and another was from Dubai. He had done a 100 miler on each continent and was now attempting to fit in as many others as he could. Then there were average Joe's like me, just doing it to see how far we could go.

The next few miles were fantastic, and as we ran through Polperro we passed several pub beer gardens that erupted in cheers. There was an amazing atmosphere that followed us along and acted like a wind upon our backs. I never slowed my pace and ran all the way to Looe, I arrived there just as the sun set. I filled my water bottles at the checkpoint and ate a power bar. Just as I set off the rain began.

Leg 2: Looe to Dobwalls, 9.3 miles, 1,429feet of climbing.

Head torch on, I set off out the back of Looe, and I was instantly plunged into dense woodland. Although the event organisers said they had marked a trail through the woods it was far from good. Only 2 miles in and I was lost. I had my map out and was studying it, however maps are useless unless you know where you are on them so back in my pack it went.

By now it was pitch black and the rain was hammering down. I put on my waterproof jacket, dug my compass out and just headed north, never easy when thousands of trees stand in your way. I carried on for a good half an hour without seeing another person when I suddenly burst out onto a muddy track and three head torches turned my way blinding me. A woman's voice piped up "Do you know the way?"

I replied "No! I'm just heading north."

All three runners, faces obscured behind the glare of their head torches replied together "So were we, until we came to this."

They turned and pointed their head torches to show me a three way split in the track. "Perfect!!!" We all decided to take the most churned up path hoping it was other runners that made it look that way. After several hundred meters we found an arrow sign. We were on the right track.

Then things got very hard, and the mud was so deep it just oozed into my trainers with every step. Twice they came off and got jammed deep in the sludge. The rain was now insane and incredibly cold. We were largely protected from the wind by the trees. Only when we found small sections of open ground did we realise just how strong the wind was. The dense foliage made it slow going and after wading through a river I was chilled to the bone.

As we entered Dobwalls one of the guys next to me was babbling rubbish. He was wreaked. We found the checkpoint and he instantly pulled out. I was surprised to find my drop bag here. I thought it was supposed to be at the next aid station: The Jamaica Inn. Then someone told me they were dropping it off here and at the Jamaica Inn as the conditions were so harsh people may need extra equipment. In it were dry clothes and food.

By now I was so cold I couldn't move my hands and I was getting dizzy. I decided not to use my dry clothes here as the section after Jamaica Inn was more exposed and I'd use them then. So I left them in the drop bag and headed for the door.

Leg 3: Dobwalls to Jamaica Inn, 9.4 miles, 1,191feet of climbing.

As I left the checkpoint I was in a hell of a state. I had my arms across my chest trying to keep warmth in. I was just coming out the top of Dobwalls when a female runner passed me. I noticed her face from a magazine cover and an ultra-running webpage, but I couldn't put a name to the face. I tried my best to keep her in sight just as a motivational goal. I managed it for about a mile before the last glows of her head torch faded and I was alone again.

The rain was still hammering down but I was now on a dirt track and protected by a hedge row from the wind. I got into a fair pace and I started to feel good again. As I went on I caught up and passed several other runners. We all exchanged greetings but everybody looked worn. Eventually I ended up on a long track and found myself in a group of 6 runners. None of us spoke. We just all plodded along in an ever changing speed march, but eventually all got into the same step and it reminded me so much of my days doing army basic training, all marching as a troop.

This went on for a good hour until each runner peeled away to waiting cars at the side of the road. People crewing them dried them off and gave them warm drinks, a luxury I didn't have. I found myself alone again for several miles until I came up behind two very friendly guys that I got chatting to. We got talking about where we were from and why we were doing something so stupid. Before I knew it we had arrived at the Jamaica Inn.

My relief at arriving here turned to complete despair when I was informed that my drop bag had been transported to the 70 mile point. I was 30.5 miles in, soaking wet and starving, with 8 miles of open moorland in front of me. The aid station only had jelly babies and water, nothing warm to drink or eat. Common sense should have seen me pull out, but I was so fuming from not seeing my drop bag I pushed on and decided to take my anger out on the moors.

Chapter 11

From Dusk until Dawn

Leg 4: Jamaica Inn to Barn Park, 8 miles, 930 feet of climbing.

I set off passing 5 cars all drying off other runners and giving them warm food. I was in a rage. I had been living on power bars and jelly babies for 7 hours now, and several of us felt like the event organisers had let us down. They had promised real food stations along the way, not a child's pick and mix. I had an emergency pasty in my bag but I chose to keep that for a dire emergency, a decision I'm so glad I made at the time.

I ran under the A30 and came to a gate that led out onto Bodmin moor. The rain was intense and driven sideways by the blasting wind. Two other runners came to the gate and we all decided to stick together through this dangerous section. As we climbed over the gate two more runners came up behind and said they would follow us. We got the compass out and took a due north reading then set off, half a mile in visibility went down to about 5 feet. The wind and rain had gotten so brutal it was hard to stand up. I turned around and the two guys behind me were no longer there. I called out to the two in front but my words were instantly blasted away by the wind.

After another 50 or so meters we came to a stop. We were falling over and ankle deep in sludge. We took a new compass bearing and set off again, but it was slow going and the wind was driving the cold into my core. I kept stumbling and I constantly saw the two guys in front of me hit the ground too. Lumps of grass, rocks and deep pools of mud that made up the moor were unseen through the driving rain. We came to a stop again, completely unsure of where we were, then we heard a whistle, distant but distinctive. We headed to it, then the light of two head torches came into view. It took a full blown shout to communicate with each other in the wind. A voice shouted but it was hardly audible "Does anyone know where we are?"

Head torches shook left and right indicating a solid "NO!"

I was now beyond the realms of cold and all I could think was "I'm stood in this dam storm wearing shorts." Two more head torches joined our group. We all huddled into a rugby type scrum to protect ourselves from the elements and got to business.

Someone said "Right, we are all in the shit, agreed?"

Everyone piped up "Agreed!!!!" I got my compass out and someone produced a map, we all decided we needed to find a way-point on the moors. Heading north was the direction we needed to go, but that had potentially 6 miles of open moorland and we would all be hypothermic by then.

We looked at the map and all decided to try to find a wall that lead from North to South through the moors. If we found that we could follow it until sun up. I glanced at my watch. It was 3:15am, about an hour and 15 minutes until sun rise. So we took a compass bearing due east and stumbled off in search of the wall. I was second in the group and we all got into the habit of checking each other every few moments. Lead guy would swing his head torch around and see me, I would turn around and see the person behind me, and they would do the same to whoever was behind them. Visibility now was only a few feet. It was like a whiteout. This went on for what felt like an eternity until lead guy stopped and shouted back "I've found the fucking wall, yes you bastard!!" We all scrambled over it and sat with our backs against it savouring a moment of being out of the wind.

The man next to me started shaking his head saying "I'm not doing this shit again, Jesus, Jesus Christ, this isn't fucking racing, this is fucking insane!" We all stood up and pushed on. The wall was low. It protected our legs from the wind but our upper bodies still took a pounding. We travelled along it for a good mile and a half crossing two knee deep streams that chilled us even further. Then we found a corner where another wall joined it. We huddled together again and all agreed that we now knew where we were on the map.

With sun up due in about 20 minutes we took a compass bearing and headed for Brown Willy, the highest point in Cornwall. As we went on, the eerie glow of morning light started to show us a hazy horizon, something to focus on through the rain. We went across a boggy field, then in front of us a hill went up and disappeared into a dense fog. We were at the foot of Brown Willy. As we climbed it, mud turned into rock and eventually we were all scrambling up a near vertical rock face. It was exhausting after being so cold for so long.

When we reached the top we all just fell to the floor, it was very foggy but light enough now to turn our head torches off. It was the first time I had gotten to see the faces of those who I had been with. They looked just how I felt: completely shattered. We got to our feet and wondered off to the trig point at the very top. We all took long swigs from our water bottles then looked at the path leading down and off the moors. An instant moment of camaraderie spread through us and we all shook hands and patted each other on the back for working together and getting through such a horrific night. None of us knew each other, but by working together we overcame and endured.

We split up and I burst into a run down the back of Brown Willy and ended up traversing several fields full of horses before eventually ending up on a huge disused airfield. I ran the full length of it until I saw a flag indicating the checkpoint. I blasted towards it, hoping for something warm to eat or drink, yet again I was bitterly disappointed. Just sweets and water. They told me the next checkpoint almost half marathon distance away was the nearest place with warm drinks. I almost collapsed from exhaustion. I had covered 39 miles with no real food. It was time for my emergency pasty. It was also at this point that I realised I had not peed in almost 11 hours - not good. I was dehydrated and risking kidney damage, so I drank a full litre of water before heading on. The rain continued to pour down.

Leg 5: Barn Park to Tintagel, 11.5 miles, 1,696feet of climbing.

I left Barn Park at exactly 6am on the Saturday morning and continued north towards the coast. I was alone for the first mile or so as I ran down country lanes looking for signs to Boscastle. I knew from the maps that cross country was still the way to go as roads in the area took a longer route.

Up ahead I saw another runner dressed in black so followed him, but little did I know at the time this was the start of a love – hate relationship that was to last 20 miles. He always remained about 50 meters in front of me, but if I tried to catch him he would speed up. This continued across several muddy fields. Eventually we came to a huge overgrown field and straight away I knew he was heading in the wrong direction. I whistled out to him and pointed him the correct way, he didn't even thank me, and this ended up happening several times. Eventually I had had enough and tried to overtake him on a grassy hill, just then we got hit by an unholy downpour. The rain was so hard it hurt my head through my hood. We still fought each other across a fast flowing stream and right to the top of the hill. Why we were racing like this a good 40 plus miles into a 100 miler was beyond me. All I knew was I didn't like him, having said that I probably wouldn't have liked anybody around me at this point in the game. As we got to the top he keeled over and got violently sick.

My determination to pass him turned to remorse and I offered him some water, but he just brushed my arm away and continued on without a word. I took a swig out of the bottle myself and just looked at his back as he ran off into a wooded area we were heading for. I uttered to myself "You ignorant bastard." I now had a mission: I was going to get past this person no matter what.

The next few miles were like a chase scene from a Hollywood thriller. I blasted after him through thick woodland trails, and the distance between us varied as we scrambled over walls and fallen logs. Seeing his back was like watching a log in the surf. He ebbed and flowed continuously, until we eventually found ourselves running alongside a large stream. Buildings started to appear at a regular rate, something I hadn't seen since leaving Dobwalls many hours earlier.

All of a sudden we were in a very picturesque village: Boscastle. I had made the north coast. Just then the rain stopped. Black clothed guy disappeared from my view around a corner as I stopped to ask a stunned but cheerful local which way to the coast path. He was a man in his mid-60s with a beaming smile on his face. "Are you one of those night runners that's on the news?" he asked. I said I didn't realise we had made the news but I could well be. He pointed across a small bridge and told me to stick to the right. His final words as I left rang in my head "You'll know when you are on the coast path because it gets rather hilly."

The instant I rounded the next corner I was confronted with a muddy path that just went skyward. My reply to his departing comment now came "No shit!!!"

I scrambled up the path and as I came to the top I was confronted by a truly incredible sight. On my right as I looked down was Boscastle and stretching off in that direction were some impressive cliffs, then as I scanned my head to the left an unimaginable set of cliffs stretched off to the horizon. They rose and fell like a giant rollercoaster. Much pain and hard work lay ahead. Then something caught my eye; black clothed guy was about half a mile away. He was traveling at a jogging pace, heading for the next headland. I was still on a mission.

I set off at a pace that surprised me. The last time I had covered this type of distance I could hardly walk, but here I was running with little discomfort, sure I had the odd ache but nothing that truly hurt. I pressed on down steep muddy descents and up rocky winding paths, and through overgrown sections that looked untouched for some time, then I caught up with my adversary. He was struggling up a set of rock steps that climbed over the next headland. I could see there was enough room to get by him so I went for it.

Yet again we were in a fight but this time I prevailed. I scrambled over the top and flat out ran down the next descent. I carried on and didn't look back for a good 10 minutes, at which time he was out of sight. This "chase" I was in completely took away the thoughts of the overall challenge and before I knew it I found myself looking upon the next headland and the next checkpoint: Tintagel Castle.

I got to the bottom of the headland that the Castle stood on and started the climb, which was up a large set of steps. It took a good 15 minutes before I found myself in the ruins at the top. As I got there it was empty, no checkpoint, and no people for that matter. I scrambled around the ruins and the whole headland for a good 15 minutes. I then dug out my mobile and called the race organisers "Emergency helpline." No answer (they never did call me back to see if I was ok). Then as I sat down wondering what to do next, I saw black clothed guy past the castle and heading towards the next headland. I climbed out of the ruins and ran after him. Over the next rise was the checkpoint, and as I got there I was informed that they had moved it due to the wind. Nice of them to inform us all.

I couldn't be bothered to be angry at them. I couldn't see red. All I could see was a steaming cup of tea in a paper cup at the back of the gazebo. I went over and helped myself to one. I put in 3 sugars in an attempt to fight off any hypoglycaemia and grabbed a handful of salted crisps that were in a bowl. Black clothed guy was just setting off as I was starting to sip my tea. I muttered under my breath "See you soon buddy."

Leg 6: Tintagel to Port Isaac, 9.3 miles, 3,076feet of climbing.

Straight out of the checkpoint I was plunged into hell. The coast path around this section was unimaginable. It literally went down to sea level then vertical again, up to 200 feet. It was incredibly hard, and it was made harder still by the weather. On the downward sections I would have a full on head wind that would periodically blast scattered showers into my eyes and chill me to the bone. On the climbs, I would be protected from the wind and would overheat. So I found myself for the next 3 hours putting on my jacket and hat as I started a descent and taking them off as I scaled another cliff. It became draining.

Black clothed guy and I swapped places many times during this stage and eventually the competition between the two of us faded to a mutual understanding. Hell, we even started nodding to each other as we passed. As we progressed along this stretch of coast we got overtaken by many runners in the 60 mile event that had started at 8am that morning. This gave us a well needed boost as they patted us on our backs and wished us good luck. Many asked "How did you get through last night? The weather was brutal." At that moment, even I couldn't answer that one.

It was towards the end of this section that I first encountered a few troubles. On one of the downward sections, I started to feel a cramp in my right calf muscle, and as hard as I tried, I could not stretch it out. I knew I probably had a sodium imbalance now due to lack of salt, but I had started peeing so at least things were working internally. Also as I looked down at my calf I noticed a blood bubble on my shin and directly over a vein, this instantly forced me to slow as I know such things can turn into a full blown aneurysm. Last thing I wanted to do was start haemorrhaging out on an exposed coast path. I kept a check on it to make sure it wasn't changing in size and after an hour I was happy that whatever it was it was temporarily localised, so I pressed on.

When I eventually rounded a cliff and saw the town of Port Isaac a lump filled my throat. After the last stage it felt emotional to see real life and structures once again. Emotion increased even more when I discovered that the checkpoint was at the very top of the highest hill there. Yet again it was just a bag of jelly babies and water. No real food after 59 miles. I was beginning to think that the race organisers were trying to kill us all off. There were eight other runners here looking very ill indeed, and three had pulled out and were waiting for pick up, the others were unsure of continuing themselves. At this point there was still no doubt in my mind that I was going to continue. Yes I was worn-out, but I still felt positive.

As I stood there about to leave, black clothed guy arrived at the aid station and instantly handed in his timing chip. His words were "That's it, no more." I was a bit gutted. I was back to fighting the course again and not another person. I set off for the next checkpoint as he collapsed on the floor.

Chapter 12

Steel Walls

Leg 7: Port Isaac to Rock, 11.6 miles, 2,465feet of climbing.

As I set off I headed directly through the town centre, stunned and bewildered onlookers staring on with mouths agape. I must have looked like a convict on the run. I was covered in mud, blood was running down my legs from bramble scratches and falling on rocks, and I was hobbling with my cramped calf.

Then something caught my eye, a sight like no other – a fish and chip shop. From the moment I saw it to bursting through its door was the fastest I had moved during the entire event. A larger than life 20 something year old lad with glasses looked at me in fear. I burst out babbling "Oh mate am I glad to see you, chips, coke, where's your coke? Full fat coke, I need caffeine, chips, tell me you're not closed?????" He tried to calm me down, not an easy task when I'm in that frame of mind. After 5 minutes of explaining to him what I was doing he handed me the largest portion of chips I had ever seen, I paid for them and gave him a few pounds bonus for the extra helping. I completely covered the chips in salt and sat on the curb outside. I must have looked like a hyena scavenging from a carcass as I tore into them. I finished the greasy feast and walked through the rest of the town drinking the coke. The two foods I try to avoid were now like a blessing from above. I came out the back end of Port Isaac feeling positively magical. This feeling however soon faded as I was plunged back into the routine of changing clothes over each headland.

I got about an hour into this section when the weather took a turn for the worse. Scattered showers became full blown continuous rain and the wind turned into a rage. Things started to come in and out of focus, and although I was making good forward progress I could no longer grasp just what I was doing. For the whole event so far I had not felt tired. I had been awake at this point for around 35 hours and in the race for 20, but now things were changing. My mind was seeking rest.

I pressed on around the coast path, but my vision started to get more tunnelled. As I entered the next town I started to see things I knew were not there. Strange spinning images like a child's hand held windmill twirled in the sky when I looked up, and as I looked at the ground it shimmered like wind over a puddle of water.

I bumbled on at a jog until I came to a long sandy beach, and although I had run past several beaches along the route this was the first time that I had to make my way directly across one. Up until now my feet had stayed in good shape against unimaginable odds, no blisters even though they had been in wet socks and muddy, gravel filled trainers since I entered the forest by Looe over 50 miles back. I tried my best not to kick up any sand as I crossed the beach but it proved impossible. By the time I left the far end of it my trainers were caked in sand and it was already grinding into my feet.

I climbed another headland only to see an even longer stretch of beach that disappeared into the distance, its end hidden by the waves of rain blowing onto the shore. I shut my mind down at this point and just tried to concentrate on putting one foot in front of the other. Although there was still plenty of strength left in my legs, my body just wouldn't let me use them to their full capacity. Things started to become a daze as I entered the next town. I had my head down against the blasting rain and just kept moving, when I looked up I was literally on top of the checkpoint. It was a lifeboat station by a small harbour.

As I entered through the boat's launch doors I was confronted by a makeshift field hospital; runners were laid up everywhere, some in blizzard bags, others curled up in a ball in a corner. There must have been 20 runners and the same number who were crewing them scattered around the building.

I went to the check in and scanned my chip. They promptly handed me my drop bag, the one I was expecting to have received at the Jamaica Inn some 50 miles back. I found a wall, rummaged through the drop bag and put on dry running gear. If anything I felt colder. I ate a pasty and two chocolate bars. I fished my phone out of my pack and headed to the main door to get a signal.

As I looked out the coast lay in front of me, I could see down towards Wadebridge, across to Padstow and around the next headland. It was being savaged by rain. My phone turned on and the image of my two sons Logan and Owen appeared on the screen, the driving force that gets me through steel walls in my life just put one up. At that instant I no longer thought of them as an inspiration to run, but more as a reason to stop. I was starting to put myself in real danger. I was hallucinating and about to head out onto an exposed coast path for another 33 miles and into a second night. Yes I could run on, yes I still had power in me, but would it be fair on them or Claire if I injured myself or worse for the sake of a medal? The answer was no. I phoned Claire and told her of my decision to stop. Ever supportive of me she said "Do whatever you think is right."

I went over to a race official and handed my chip in. He told me I looked the strongest one there, but I insisted. At the moment he took it off my wrist I fell against the wall and slid to the floor. The fight had left me. I didn't realise just how much my mind had been holding my body up. I was instantly exhausted. One minute I was standing, the next I found it hard to crawl back to my drop bag.

As I waited for Claire to pick me up more people came into the checkpoint. They looked wreaked. Did I honestly look that bad? I must have. I sat there and let my mind go back over what I had done. 21 hours earlier I had been running along the south coast in blazing sunshine, and since then I had pushed through miles of woodland, crossed Bodmin moor at night in outrageous conditions, fought my way to the coast and overcome the harshest cliffs in Cornwall, all on minimum food. I had travelled 71 miles, climbed 13,048 feet and not slept in 36 hours, as I thought back I couldn't help but smile that I had gotten as far as I had.

Claire arrived 2 hours later to pick me up, and when she did she had to support me as I hobbled to her car. My legs had completely ceased up. The days following the UTSW were the most painful post event wise I have ever felt, and I was forced to crawl up and down stairs, and couldn't even get in my car to drive. I also ate constantly, even in the early hours of the morning. I would wake at 2 or 3am, slide down the staircase on my behind and raid the fridge.

Here I am some 8 years later writing this and thinking back to the events of that weekend. Although I know I made the right decision to stop, I still wonder just how much further I could have continued. Doing events like these and pushing the boundaries with my running, I continue to learn more and more about myself physically and mentally. I thrive on seeing just what I can get through and how far I can push my mind and body, and I'm glad that I found a point at which I know when to stop.

Although I did not finish the UTSW, it is still one of the races I am most proud of, my memories of that event are a bigger reward than any medal I would have received for completing it. We all go through times in our lives that change us, we encounter moments of hardships and loss, or ones of elation and happiness, but they mould us into the person we are. Not finishing the UTSW showed me that no matter what age I shall live to, I will always keep on learning about myself and my true potential. There are ultra runners who would have completed the UTSW in 24 hours or less, but I am not one of them and I never will be. I am just an average person with average abilities that wants to see what I can achieve without taking these events too seriously. I am merely finding the limits.

Yet again, as I recovered from the pains of the race, I wanted to go back for more, however it was not fair on Claire to continue with the level of training I was putting in, especially with our two boys being so very young, so I went back to doing 10k's and the odd half marathon. This was far from the end of my endurance adventures however, as something happened that would not only see me doing large events again, but ones that would take me back to my military roots.

A tragic event was reported on the news 3 weeks after I took part in in the UTSW that would directly affect the races I participated in 2 years later. On 13th July, 2013. Edward Maher, aged 31, Craig Roberts, aged 24, and James Dunsby, aged 31, died on SAS (Special Air Service) selection. They collapsed during a test march in the Brecon Beacons when temperatures reached 29.5C (85F). Their loss was not just a devastating blow to their families and friends, but also to the Special Air Service Regiment itself.

In 2014 ex and serving Special Forces soldiers staged an event in their honour, that not only involved military personnel but civilians too – The Fan Dance. For those who have no military knowledge what so ever, most picture the Fan Dance as colourfully decorated ladies dancing around waving fans. However for those that have any knowledge of the Special Forces, they will know it is a hard military selection march in the Brecon Beacons that goes over the summit of its highest mountain, Pen-y-fan (hence the name Fan Dance).

The event was such a success that the soldiers who organised it put together a company called The Special Forces Experience (TSFE). They came to realise that many of the general public (like myself) have a passion for challenges and adventure, and we all wish to see just how far we can push ourselves.

In 2014 TSFE announced that they would give a select few civilians the chance to do three of the SAS selection tests set by the regiment. The three tests are - Special Forces 10 (SF10), Fan Dance, and Point to Point (P2P): the march that the three soldiers perished on. Participants could either do each march as an individual event, or try to complete all three in strict time limits and go on to earn a Loadstone medal. A portion of the proceeds raised from the events would go to a charity picked by the families of the soldiers who died (they chose Talking Minds, a charity that helps those suffering from post-traumatic stress disorder).

Upon hearing of these events I mentioned them to Claire and she said I should go for them, so I applied straight away for the Loadstone category. Unfortunately I had missed the event deadline for Loadstone in 2014, however I secured a place for the following year. The first Loadstone event SF10 was to be on 2nd of May 2015. I would then do one each month until I failed one or completed them all. For me this was the mother lode of all events, not just for the challenge and adventure this time, but for something far harder to explain. What the SAS has represented to me over the years is the true pinnacle of excellence, not just in the world of soldiering, but in how they overcome obstacles no matter what they are, and they pull through. I have done countless marches over the years during and after my time in the military, but to do the SAS selection marches is any ex or serving soldier's dream.

So as soon as I found out I had acquired a place on the courses I was out the door, running over Dartmoor with boots and Bergan again. However after several outings, I knew the only way to get back into the feel of military marches is to do a real one. After asking a few royal marine friends for ideas they gave me the name of a guy who also held a Fan Dance march in the Brecon Beacons.

After a bit of research I found the guy they were speaking of and the adventure company he ran. His name was Ken Jones, and his background was an interesting one. After 4 years in the parachute regiment and 2 years in the SAS reserves, Ken got hit by an avalanche while attempting a solo climb to a mountain summit in Romania. He broke his hip and femur, and it took him 4 days to crawl off the mountain to safety. It then took him a further 2 years to learn to walk again, however he is now (as I discovered on this event) back to full health. He wrote a book of his avalanche experience titled Darkness Descending.

So I put myself in for his Winter Fan Dance event carrying full SAS loadbearing weight (50lbs), as a training exercise build up to Loadstone.

Chapter 13

Brecon Bleakons

On Friday January 9th 2015, I found myself leaving Devon and driving north on the M5. I knew the weather over the weekend was going to be a mixture of heavy rain and gales, with the possibility of snow over the hills, and as I drove across the Severn Bridge into Wales the weather report didn't disappoint. I was being blown from one side of the carriageway to the other, and my car was like a plastic bag in a breezy shop doorway. By the time I started driving through the Brecon Beacons, the driving rain was practically apocalyptic.

I got hopelessly lost on mountain roads due to lack of signs, land marks, and internet connection. I only found my eventual destination by having lengthy phone conversations with Claire, who was trying to triangulate my location on the computer at home while I described where I was.

The Fan Dance event for the SAS starts at a place called the Storey Arms on the A470 in Wales, and has done so for about 30 years. Out the front of it resides what is described in many military literature books as "the world's most famous telephone box." An old red telephone box that marks the start and finish point of most of the Special Forces test marches.

Upon getting out of my car on arrival I didn't think I'd have to climb the mountain, I thought the wind would blow me up it and right off the top. It was brutal, and as I carried my kit to the registration point, I renamed the place the Brecon Bleakons.

Registration consisted of a queue much like you find on one of the rides at a theme park. There were around 150 to 200 people dressed like they were ready to go into combat, and in a way we all were, but the enemy this time was against the hills, the weather, and our determination to get the job done. I spent an hour being buffeted around by event staff and competitors like I was at the mercy of a pin ball machine.

After getting my Bergan weighed and doing several checks, it was back to my accommodation for the night – my car. Hotels and places to stay in the local area were very scarce indeed so I had no choice. Back seats down and sleeping bag out I was ready for a cold night, but just as I was getting settled a tap came at my side window. I wound it down to find a huge head push its way in through the rain. It was a police officer. In his broad Welsh accent he blurted out "Arrrre you sleepin' in eeerr tonight? If so dooon't you gooo wuuunderin around oooutside, you will die if you goo intooo the mountains." I gave him my reassurances that I had no wish to do such a stupid thing, and he left me to it.

A Skoda Fabia at night in the Bleakons is not a fun place to be, let me tell you. I was cramped in the back in the foetal position with three layers on and a double sleeping bag over me, and I was still feeling cold. Sleet, then snow at one point, was blasting against the windows.

Between the hours of 1am and 3am I felt like I was in a washing machine, the car was rocking so much. In between it all though I did find a few hours' sleep.

As the morning approached, I was starting to get into the "mode". I was checking all my equipment again and again just to make sure I was prepared for every eventuality. The start of the event was at 8am but we all arranged to be at the old red telephone box at 7:45am. I kitted myself out in full army Gortex for the start. I knew I would be waiting around for a good 15 minutes before the start so didn't want to compromise myself heat wise before the off.

As we all gathered together the weather came to a screaming climax. It was absolutely howling. The ever growing crowd moved as a group and glided against each other like a colony of Emperor Penguins, each one of us taking it in turn to ride the chills of the outside edge of the huddle.

Eventually 8 o'clock came and Ken pushed his way to the middle of the group with another member of the DS (Directing Staff) for a quick briefing. He outlined the most hazardous parts of the 15 mile route and the weather conditions expected over the coming hours. He informed us that although conditions were better the other side of Pen-y-fan, the temperature was going to drop as the day went on and snow was due by the evening. He finished with the words "For your courageous decision in committing to this Special Forces event you have all set yourself apart from the crowd. We are not looking for heroes or record breakers. The characteristics we look for are self-motivation, determination, courage, self-belief, pride, respect for your fellow participants and a mind-set that will not allow you to give in. You will be embarking upon a pilgrimage and following in the footsteps of a history of young men who have been in search of something out of the ordinary. Who Dares Wins!"

Inspiring words that completely hushed us all and brought an even deeper meaning to the challenge ahead.

There was no starter pistol or signal to go, the group just all moved off up the first hill into a single line, every face etched with the determination of a man on a mission. The hill on which we start is a good 400 meters of vertical climb. It was exhausting right from the first step. The wind was blasting the rain horizontally into us and the noise of it was deafening. However I actually felt quite good. I was soaking wet, the 50lbs in my Bergan felt crushingly heavy, yet I was coping really well, and within 10 minutes the effort of the climb warmed me up nicely. I was slightly heartbroken at the top of the hill though when I looked down at my Garmin and it read that I had only travelled 0.4 of a mile. When moving over steep or uneven ground carrying weight, it's hard to judge just how far you have travelled.

At the top we all took our turn to shuffle through a kissing gate and headed across to the valley beyond.

Me at the start of the winter Fan Dance, 2014.

As we approached it, the view was staggering. Through the low clouds I could see down to a stream at the bottom and across to a hill that went vertical: the ascent to Pen-y-fan.

Here I broke into a run. Avoiding large rocks and areas of slippery mud, I pushed myself right to the bottom of the hill. The thin line that appeared as a stream at the top was actually a fast flowing, knee deep torrent. There were several large boulders in it that I used as stepping-stones so as not to completely submerge my boots. As I leapt off the last one I toppled over like a drunk and fell side down in sludgy mud. I had a quick laugh at myself and pressed on.

This next ascent was very tough indeed, and everybody was spreading out now as we all found the pace that suited us. I got into my own little bubble and just focused on the ground in front of me, watching where I placed every step and making sure not to slip.

The wind and rain didn't let up. I continued on climbing for about 20 minutes when up ahead I saw a person dressed in black with a pack on facedown at the side of the track. There was another person bent over them. I rushed up to see if all was ok. The crouched over figure pulled his hood back and shouted through the wind, "They just went down in front of me." I bent down and helped him roll the prone person over.

It was a young woman of about 25, her blond hair matted across her face. I shouted out for a response but got nothing back. I put my ear next to her mouth to check she was breathing, her breath was shallow but very rapid. Her head rolled to one side and she looked totally lifeless.

I looked at the other guy and asked if he knew who she was, and he said no.

She showed no obvious signs of injury from falling over so we both bent her forward to take her pack off. The first golden rule of anyone going down in the hills or mountains is – shelter them from the elements. You also use the equipment they have on themselves first (if they have any) not your own, otherwise you compromise your own safety.

I could see the other guy was switched on straight away. He was using mine and his own Bergan, which we had taken off to create a wind break for her while I checked her pack for a shelter.

There was only a very small sleeping bag in a compression sack about the size of a house brick, and a flimsy foil blanket, both totally useless in the conditions we were experiencing. I did however find an asthma inhaler which instantly sent alarm bells ringing in my head.

I went straight to my Bergan to retrieve my blizzard bag, something I always carry with me no matter what I do outdoors. They are small but completely wind and waterproof. I swapped pleasantries with the other guy as we got her into the blizzard bag, and he told me his name was Ian. I used her pack to support her on one side as close to the recovery position as the blizzard bag would allow, as Ian got on his phone trying to raise the alarm. We both tried but there was no signal.

The next guy up the hill ran over to us and asked if we needed help. We gave him the basics of what had happened and he then took off his Bergan to add to her wind break. At that point she started to murmur. I bent over and asked her what her name was, it took a few attempts but eventually I heard a whispered "Natalie." I quizzed her about the inhaler and showed it to her. She instantly tried to reach out for it, so I gave it to her. I then spotted two competitors fully kitted out in combat gear coming up the rise. I saw aerials coming out of the top of their Bergans, which meant they carried a two way radio. Ian helped Natalie with her inhaler as I ran to the guys coming up. After a very quick brief of the situation they tried to call both RV1 just past the summit of Pen-y-fan and base camp (Storey Arms) at the bottom, but they themselves drew a blank signal wise. After a quick discussion they said they would press on to higher ground to try and acquire a signal and alert Ken and the DS (Directing Staff) at base camp.

I went back over to Ian and informed him and the other man that had stopped, that the radio guys were going to try to call in help from further up. Over the next 15 minutes we all kept talking to Natalie and jokingly tried to keep spirits high. She started responding well and answered our questions quickly. I however was starting to get very, very cold. My lack of movement and the constant wind chilled me to the bone. Ian and the other guy were visibly shaking too.

We all decided that the best thing to do to speed the process up was for one of us to run back to base camp and get help. Ian said he was happy to stick with Natalie if the other two of us ran back down for help. We all agreed. It was Bergans on and off we went.

We set off at an absolutely blistering pace, one I never thought I had in me, not with combat boots on and carrying the weight I was. We crossed the stream and climbed the next rise without breaking stride, then blasted down the first hill back to the start line.

We made our way around to the back of the Storey Arms and burst into the main office. Ken and three other DS were all around a table looking at a map.

I explained the situation and Natalie's location. They all sprang straight into action. Ken was instantly on the radio to RV1, and the other three went through a side door and reappeared with Bergans. One of which I knew was a medical evacuation pack. They started to have a rapid discussion amongst themselves of the best way to tackle the location where she was, when simultaneously me and the guy I'd ran back with said we were willing to go back up and help if need be.

Ken looked at us then instantly blasted out his plan, "Good, that means we won't have to pull a man down from RV1."

I made the decision to ditch my Bergan and grab my combat jacket. As we all headed past the old red telephone box and up the first ascent again, Ken and the other two DS took the lead. This was the first time I had a proper chance to talk to the guy I'd ran back with. He told me his name was Mark and he came from Bedfordshire.

As we talked he asked me how I felt about not finishing the event because of what had happened. Up until that time I never thought about it. I suppose from the moment I took my blizzard bag out and compromised my own pack I secretly knew it was over. Yet I wasn't bothered. Say if I had pushed on and ignored that a person was down, then I found out later that they had perished because no one helped, could I have lived with myself? Hell no.

I explained to him that I have two young sons, and if they were in trouble at the side of a track somewhere I'd like to think that someone would help them too. He went on to tell me that his daughter was in this race non-loadbearing, and he thought exactly the same thing. We both pressed on up the hill and down into the next valley.

We crossed the stream and I could see up ahead that Ken and the two DS were with Natalie and Ian. As we approached they helped her to her feet. She was more switched on now, but still in what they say in the forces as "shit-state." She was pasty white and wobbly on her feet. However she was talking with confidence and trying to do things for herself. I left the DS to check her over as I took in the view.

The wind was still howling, but the rain had stopped, and the sun was doing its best to shine through. It painted the hills around us with different shades of green and golden brown. The Brecon's are harsh, but they certainly don't lack in beauty.

After a few minutes we all set off back down to base camp. We all thought it best to keep Natalie on her feet for as long as possible, keeping her temperature up by generating heat by movement. Each of us took it in turns supporting her and then we carried her across the stream.

As we were about to start the next ascent, Mark said he was going to head back up to RV1 past the summit to see if he could catch up with his daughter on her way back down. We shook hands and I gave him my emergency supply of food from my pockets and water from my belt. He left with a wink of the eye and a beaming smile.

We all came up over the rise and then started our descent back to the start point. Natalie was surrounded by Ken and the DS like they were bodyguards protecting a client.

I moved out in front and got chatting to Ian. Ian was an instantly likable guy. He was around my age, 40ish, with fading hair like mine, and a laugh that sounded like a hacking cough. I asked him what brought him here. He replied by saying he had acquired a place on something called Loadstone. My ears shot up. I told him that I too was also down for that formidable challenge.

Back at the Storey Arms I shook Ian's hand and told him I looked forward to seeing him again at the start of Loadstone in May.

Natalie was brought through and sat in a chair in the main office. She still looked ghastly, but she managed a fleeting smile and thanked me for my help. I left her with the DS and headed for my car.

Ken caught up with me outside and offered me something hot to drink. I said I had a long drive ahead of me and would like to start getting back to Plymouth. He then said he would secure me a place on next year's event for free.

I did stay on for a good half an hour chatting to various hikers and runners who were outside the Storey Arms. I mentioned other endurance races I'd competed in and they savagely interrogated me on what I carried and ate over long distances. I could see their brains ticking over like so many other endurance people I've talked to in the past, always eager to know what works for others and to see if anything new can be learned to benefit themselves. Eventually I headed for my car and the long drive home.

I felt slightly numb that I didn't complete the event, yet knew that it was for the best. No patch or medal is more important than a life.

When I got back home that evening I saw a message on a Facebook page linked to the event that brought a lump to my throat, "The mental and physical strength it takes to arrive at a start line of an event like this cannot be measured. However that also cannot compare to what it takes to give up the finish line to help another person in need of aid. To the three that helped extract the casualty from Pen-y-fan today we give our thanks. Not by strength, by guile. Who Dares Wins!" That made it all worthwhile. With the start of Loadstone only 15 weeks away, this was just the beginning of my adventures in the Brecon Beacons.

Chapter 14

Loadstone

I quickly recovered from my disappointment of not completing the winter Fan Dance and just carried on training as before. I spent more time on Dartmoor though, running up hills such as Sheepstor. I also started going out carrying heavier loads. Claire called me crazy when she saw me putting house bricks in my Bergan before I went out running with it. I have stated many times in earlier chapters how I was more suited to running with weight than being fast, however that was over 10 years previously. I was in my early 40s now and not the spring chicken I used to be.

On one Facebook page, comments started flying around about how people of my age shouldn't be allowed to enter events such as Loadstone, because we were "over the hill" and risked injuring ourselves, thus putting pressure on emergency services that would have to transport us off the mountains. This pissed me right off, and I was more determined than ever to show those who thought that way what people of my age can achieve.

I started setting my alarm for 3:30am, just so I could get up and fit in several hours of training before starting work. It was exhausting but it started paying off, and after several weeks my body adapted to carrying heavy loads again and the training runs became easier.

The weeks flew by and before I knew it SF10 was upon me. Being The Special Forces Experience (TSFE) is staffed entirely by former and serving members of the Special Forces, they take security very seriously, so they did not provide the exact locations and timings of events until near to the time. When I did receive the SF10 details I saw that it was to be held in North Wales, and for Loadstone participants it would be a 2 day affair. Day 1 would consist of field craft and navigational lessons, and day 2 would be the SF10 test march.

In the days before the event I checked my equipment again, and again. Although I had been on countless military exercises over the years, the last thing I wanted to do was suffer the embarrassment of forgetting a vital bit of equipment and appearing to be unprepared.

On 1st May 2015 I found myself driving up to Caerwys, a small town near Mold in North Wales. It was a truly draining drive which took me 6 hours from Plymouth. I will not give precise locations of "The Farm" where I was to rendezvous with TSFE, however our directions from the A55 were cryptic to say the least. I was told to count how many telephone poles I had to drive under before making a turning, etc. I certainly knew when I had found the location however, as there are not many farms with a high level of security staff surrounding them all dressed in combat gear.

I was guided through to a large field with high fences and told to set up camp. I got my small trusty two man dome tent out that had been a loyal friend since childhood and made myself at home. Several other participants arrived too and started setting up their own tents around me. I got talking to a few of them, two of which I would get to know well over the course of Loadstone. (I do not wish to state their full names so will call them RL, and AB.)

RL was a former assault pioneer and had applied for the SAS reserves in the past, however he experienced an injury on selection. AB was a mountain bike enthusiast who enjoyed adventure racing and challenges. The evening went swiftly and I was exhausted from the drive so retired to my tent quite early. It was mighty chilly and a drizzle that had been present since I arrived turned to full blown rain. Our location in the Clwydian Range is renowned for bad weather, and it didn't disappoint. The rain in the night was biblical, and my tent, which was far from suited to those conditions, fast became water logged. I closed my eyes and tried to sleep but it was impossible. I could feel the water under my sleeping bag and hear it sloshing around, but I was too cold to get out and do anything about it.

I must have finally fallen asleep in the early hours of the morning. I woke at sunrise in what can only be described as a child's swimming pool. The water in my tent was a good inch deep. I was so thankful that I left my Bergan and equipment in my car. I splashed my way to the tent opening and unzipped it,

133

then gazed out at a truly miserable day. The sky was heavy with grey clouds, and the air temperature was frigid.

Years of experience have taught me that in such situations it is important to get dry and quick, otherwise you just end up sitting there feeling sorry for yourself. So I jogged to my car and put dry gear on, then started my camping stove to get a morning brew on the go. TSFE did provide hot food, which was an absolute dream in those conditions, and as more people emerged from their tents we all made our way to a large burger van at the far side of the field.

After a well needed breakfast of sausage and bacon baps we were gathered together under a large gazebo by the DS (Directing Staff) for an event briefing. We were introduced to all the DS who were ex or serving military staff and given an outline of what the weekend, and the rest of Loadstone, would involve. Due to the extreme nature of the events and the hazardous environments in which they were to take place - i.e. mountains - we had to prove we were not going to put ourselves or those around us in danger. So day one would consist of various lessons on first aid, emergency procedures and, most importantly, navigation.

Although I had spent many years repeatedly going over these skills, I was more than happy to brush up on them again. The day fast became a blur of going from one large gazebo to another learning survival techniques and doing various physical exercises dished out by the DS. Having a military background I was used to this, however some were not and they found the whole experience daunting. This I found surprising, after all we were doing a simulated Special Forces selection course, what the hell did they expect? A Jacuzzi?

The rain never gave up for the entire day, and as the afternoon progressed the wind increased dramatically. This became slightly comical when trying to do map reading on an exposed field, I was watching a few fellow participants chase their fleeing maps as they took flight in the gusts. I must say though the navigation instruction was exceptional. That was due to the instructor who was a 25 year veteran of 22 SAS. His name was BP. This was the first time I had met him, but little did I know at the time I would go on to receive specialist tactical military training from him in the future.

As the evening approached the DS told us that we would be travelling to the location of where we were going to start the following day's test march. We were to travel there in our own cars and practice moving in convoy. We were also told to try to be inconspicuous. AB offered to drive RL and me in his car, thus cutting down on taking three cars. Even with car sharing however 20 plus cars pulled away in convoy, and all chance of being inconspicuous went out of the window as we snaked through the countryside of North Wales like a presidential motorcade.

We arrived at our location which was a small car park on a very exposed hillside. There was a large valley below us and the wind was absolutely savage. The DS gathered us all together and told us we were going to take a leisurely stroll up the track, where we would start the following morning, to our first checkpoint - Moel Famau, the highest hill in the Clwydian Range.

The group of us, which must have numbered into the 30s, set off at a steady walk and just got chatting. The wind was brutal but it was a pleasant experience and it was a nice wind down from such a full on day. It was also good to get talking with the other participants. Bonds were formed early and it became obvious even then who the determined ones of the group were.

We spent a short time in the Jubilee Tower ruins which are at the top of Moel Famau, then headed back down to the cars. The drive back in convoy was a hilarious experience. Trying to be inconspicuous in a 20 car convoy at night with lights on is impossible. Normally quiet country lanes were suddenly brought to life as we passed by like a road train. Dog walkers and pedestrians stood by at the side of the roads wondering what the hell was going on as we all passed in unison. AB, RL, and I were laughing at the insanity of it.

Arriving back at the farm the weather reached a new climax, and when I got to my tent, or more appropriately what was left of my tent, I knew I was in for a rough night. The wind and rain had crushed my inadequate dome shelter into a sorry mess of canvas and broken poles. I gathered it all together and put it in a bin nearby. I then put the seats down in my car and set up my sleeping bag in there. The weather through the night

was insane, and I was wondering how I would fair out in it the
following morning.

RL, me, and AB, receiving a briefing from the DS.

After a very restless night rocking in the car as the wind
buffeted it around, I started getting my gear together for the
march ahead. Thankfully the rain had stopped, but the wind
however was still blowing a gale. Full combat dress and boots
on, I had breakfast then drove to the start. Upon arriving there
we were given another briefing and a telling off for leaving the
farm in a mess. I knew from prior experience this is just a
military ploy to try to break your spirit, and to weed out the
weak. We were all told to do press-ups and other physical
activities as a punishment.

Those doing Loadstone were then issued with an orange cover for their Bergan, and a house brick. Weapons could not be carried by us civilians so the brick represented the rifle carried by those going through SF selection. We were told to treat it like a weapon and never to have it more than an arm's reach away. We were then told we were going to do a few warm up exercises, but these turned out to be a test in themselves.

I don't know the actual number of those who started Loadstone. It was around 30, however some failed to even complete the warm up. We had several old style military stretchers that had to be carried between us. Each had jerry cans on full of water. They were heavy and they were very awkward. We set off up the hill towards Moel Famau with the stretchers on our shoulders and we each took it in turns to swap over. I wasn't expecting anything too exhausting before the actual start of the march and still had a full combat jacket on over my other gear. I was literally boiling after a few minutes.

Unlike the regular army and the Commando reserves, the DS did not shout at us to give encouragement, but simply said "If you cannot motivate yourself to do the task then you are not Special Forces material."

Two guys fell at the wayside by the time this "warm-up" was over. The DS ran us ragged for a good half hour before taking us back to the start for the actual test march.

We were informed that the march was an out and back route over Moel Famau, across the Clwydian Range, to Moel Arthur fort, then back again. There would be checkpoints along the way to ensure our safety, and to test us on certain things such as navigation to ensure we stayed switched on mentally under pressure.

AB and I being "warmed up" by the DS.

We all set off in a three rank squad, and the DS lead us most of the way to Moel Famau, and varied our marching from fast to slow. We were even told to turn around and march backwards at one point. This was to ensure we were all warmed up for the hills ahead. When we were finally released to go on our way it was a relief, as I like going at my own pace and not having it dictated by others.

We all spread out quite quickly and within no time I found myself alone. The landscape was like a moonscape, boulders large and small littered the hillside, and valleys dropped away either side of me as I made my way across the Clwydian Range. The wind was still savage and sudden gusts would sporadically catch my Bergan from the side, sending me in a semi spin as I ran. Knowing that my Bergan was to be weighed at some point during the march to ensure I had the minimum weight of 45lbs, I carried extra weight to ensure I was over this limit even without water and food. Right from the start, my pack was crushing me and the wind made it worse.

I got into my concentration mode early on and took each section at a time focusing on the next hill or the next large boulder and making that my target. I made the first checkpoint and was asked a few questions by the DS to ensure I was coping, then let through to go on to the next one. To be honest I was surprised at how well I was doing. It had been 10 years since I did anything like this. Obviously I had been training with weight, but it is always different when you are being observed by others and under pressure to meet deadlines.

I pressed on and boulder covered hills gave way to grassy ones, then in the distance I was confronted with Moel Arthur – the half way point. Basically it looks like a giant mound of dirt covered in bracken, on top of which a fort resides. I carried on towards it and it just kept growing in size. I descended into a valley and only then did I realise the true scale of Moel Arthur: it was huge. I stopped for a moment to take it in, and when I focused I could see a small wall at the bottom of it and tiny orange dots spread up the side of the hill. They were the orange covers that were on the Bergans of those doing Loadstone.

I jogged on to the wall at the bottom of Moel Arthur and was met by a member of the DS, who yet again checked to make sure I was ok and fit for the climb ahead. I then crawled on my hands and knees through a hole in the wall and looked up. I was confronted by a near vertical hillside completely covered in thick bracken and brambles. It was a truly heart-breaking and brutal climb, and I had to stop several times to get my breath. I can only describe it as scaling a ladder made of thorns. I dread to think about what it would have been like to slip and tumble down it. By the time I made the top I was wobbling on my legs and utterly breathless.

There was a small group in front of me and when I moved over to them I realised they were gathered around a member of the DS who was weighing their Bergan's. When I took mine off I felt like I was going to float away, as the weight had been so crushing. The DS weighed it and informed me it was 54lbs, 9lbs over the minimum limit. He made a note of the weight and I was released to carry on. The way down from Moel Arthur was a lot more pleasant than the way up: it was a gentle winding path that descended to the valley below.

The torturous Moel Arthur climb.

As I set off back along the route toward the finish, I felt the all too familiar feeling of exhaustion and dizziness. I took my Bergan off and dug out my ever present emergency pasty that had saved me many times before. I sat on a rock eating it and took in the landscape around me. The wind was still gusting and making the long grass dance in a hypnotic rhythm. It had also blown away the dark clouds and the sun was casting down long beams of light into the valleys below. When the light glided across the valley floor, it would pass over fields and they would glow in their colours. Greens, browns, and yellows mixed together like paint on an artist's easel. The Special Forces may use places like this to test potential soldiers and push them to their limits, but they truly are beautiful locations, and I cherish my time in such places.

I continued on and it gradually became harder and harder, so much so that I had to compose myself as I approached a DS at a checkpoint. I did not want them to see just how tough I was finding it. The push back up to Moel Famau and the last checkpoint was immensely tough, the wind was deafening, and it was blasting right into my face. When I encountered the DS there he patted me on the back and simply said the words "Well done my man, we've all been there."

From there it was all downhill to the end. When I realised I was in shot of the finish I upped my pace and did a confident jog to the line. Little did the directing staff know just how broken I was. I went through a gate and was greeted by the director of TSFE, Mr JB. He shook my hand and congratulated me on finishing.

Although I had passed many military training courses over the years including the all arms commando course, being part of Loadstone felt special. I was a civilian now, yet a camaraderie existed amongst us all that were doing the event, one I hadn't felt since being in the forces. Going through tough and trying times with like-minded people creates strong bonds, ones that last a life time. We all stood there at the finish swapping tales of how we had gotten on through the day, and congratulated others as they came in through the gate. I was knackered but I felt brilliant inside.

After the last person came in the DS gathered all those on Loadstone together and called out the names of who had passed or failed. On that first test alone our number had dwindled. RL, AB, and I however had made the cut along with 20 plus others, and were through to the next stage - the Fan Dance - which was due to be run in 4 weeks' time.

I was presented with my SF10 medal and completion certificate, and I drove back to Plymouth a very happy and proud man, and I eagerly awaited my next adventure with TSFE at Pen-y-Fan.

Chapter 15

Fan Dance

I stayed in touch with AB an RL from SF10 and we all arranged to meet up at the Storey Arms the night before the Fan Dance event. After the disaster I had with my tent up in North Wales I opted to sleep in my car this time, and when I arrived at the Storey Arms I found that RL and AB had gone for that option too.

It was early June and the weather was slightly more pleasant than the previous month, however we were in the Brecon Beacons and conditions can change very quickly. We all parked up opposite the Storey Arms, made tea on our camping stoves and just chatted about different events and races we had done in the past. I didn't mention my failed winter Fan Dance as I didn't want to curse the following day's event. As the evening went on and darkness descended, I retired to my car which I had now christened "The Hotel Skoda" as I was starting to sleep in it on such a regular basis.

It stayed dry through the night and there was no wind. This was the first time I had actually turned up to an event and the weather was on my side. I slept well and was only woken when other Fan Dance participants started arriving in the morning and parking their cars by mine.

The DS had told us we were to meet up in the field behind the famous red telephone box for the pre-race briefing and to get our Bergan's weighed. All of us on Loadstone quickly found each other and started swapping pleasantries. I had only met these people on SF10, however I got on so well with everyone of them, we chatted like we had known each other for years. It was a far bigger crowd this time around as many others were doing the route as a one off event and not part of the Loadstone series. We on Loadstone sat around in a circle and JB, the event director, gave us the race briefing. We were also told the cut off times for completing the event if we were to go for a Loadstone medal.

There were 3 Loadstone medal categories up for grabs – Tiers 1 to 3. Tier 1 being for regular 22 SAS, tier 2 for SAS reserves, and tier 3 for regular green army pass standard. I personally didn't expect to get anywhere near the cut off times to receive any of these Loadstone medals, I just wanted to complete the event and get the basic Fan Dance medal.

Sitting there in the circle I looked up and noticed a face I had seen on the news, it was David Dunsby, the father of James Dunsby, one of the three SAS recruits that had died on selection. He was giving an interview to a TV crew. It brought back to me the reason we were all there; to honour those who lost their lives in these mountains going for their dream of being Special Forces soldiers in one of the most famous regiments in the world. We were all then asked to stand while a bugler preformed the last post. The crowd fell silent and all that could be heard were the notes from the bugle as they drifted over the hillside. It sent shivers down my spine and it made me think, not just of the three that had lost their lives on selection, but all those who had given the ultimate sacrifice for our freedom over the years.

As start time approached, the weather as usual began to take a turn for the worse, drizzle started and hail even fell briefly. All those on Loadstone were assembled in a three rank group with our bricks in hand and an orange cover over the top of our Bergan's again to show which category we were in. Then we were sent on our way up the hill towards Pen-y-Fan.

This first climb I remembered well from being there in winter, but I tried to push that last experience behind me and concentrate on getting the job done. We all arrived at the top of this ascent and swiftly descended into the valley the other side. Thankfully the small stream at the bottom wasn't a fast flowing torrent that day like back in January. I quickly ran across it and started my ascent up towards the summit. I passed where I had helped Natalie back in the winter Fan Dance and pushed on to unknown territory. Although still cloudy, the weather stayed dry and I found myself sweating heavily as I made my way up the seemingly endless climb. The views were amazing though and they took my mind off the toil I was going through.

Towards the summit of Pen-y-Fan, there was a bit of actual climbing where I did have to scramble up and over a small rock face/feature. The top of the Fan is a large flat area with a pile of small boulders on top of which the peak marker rests, stating its height: 886m.

Summit of Pen-y-Fan.

I quickly moved on and headed towards the other side and the descent down what is known as Jacob's Ladder. I had read about Jacob's Ladder many times over the years in military literature, and it is never mentioned of fondly. The view from the top was truly spectacular and it took my breath away. I could see down Jacob's Ladder and across the valley/saddle below that separated Pen-y-Fan from the next peak across – Cribyn. I started my descent, which was largely out of my control. The weight in my Bergan dug into my shoulders every step I took and I struggled to stay up right as I stumbled helplessly down the rock steps that made up Jacob's Ladder.

At the bottom I was met by a member of the DS who acknowledged me with a nob of his head. Slight confusion was caused here. All participants were issued a small laminated map at the race briefing. It showed a contour map of the local area. There was a marked line on the map that indicated the Fan Dance route. I could see the orange covers on the Bergans of other Loadstone participants climbing Cribyn, however the map indicated that we should skirt around the bottom of it. I showed it to the DS and asked him which way I should go, but he simply pointed to the summit of Cribyn.

Slightly miffed by this and wondering why we were not following the mapped route I followed the others and started climbing Cribyn. It was another ball-aching slog to the top by which time I was gasping for breath and wobbly. I caught up with two Loadstoners in front of me and we descended the back side of Cribyn together, where we were met by another member of the DS.

This DS however was not amused. He asked why we had gone over the top of Cribyn and not skirted around the bottom like the map had shown. I explained that I was directed that way by the DS at the previous checkpoint. To be honest going over Cribyn was far harder than skirting the flat section around it, and an extra bit of physical effort I could have done without.

After Cribyn we were confronted with a very long path called the Roman Road. It is about 2 meters wide and completely covered in small rocks and boulders, and I absolutely hated it! I was constantly tripping over and catching my feet on rocks. It took me about an hour to get down this section and by the time I got to the turnaround point, I was very pissed off.

I confirmed my name with the DS at the checkpoint who were fantastic. They asked several questions to ensure we were all ok. I quickly topped my water up and set off for my return journey down the Roman Road. It was even worse going back along it as my legs were now tiring and I was tripping over even more. Every swear word imaginable was heard in those hills that day.

By the time I got back to Cribyn I was livid. I had a quick chat with the DS there who made sure I went around the outside this time and not over the top, then went on my way. I was very tired by this point and my Bergan was crushing me. I knew however it was about to get worse, a lot worse, as Jacob's Ladder was just around the bend.

Looking up from the bottom of Jacob's Ladder is actually deceiving. Although the climb looks steep and high, it doesn't look far to the top – until you start to climb up it.

The further up you go the steeper it becomes and the further away the top appears. There is also a slight ridge, so when you think you are near the top you see over the ridge and realise that the actual summit is a very long way up still. Jacob's Ladder is a true physical and mental challenge and I can see why they use it on Special Forces selection. Even if you want to just give up you still have to make it to the top to do so as there is nowhere else to go. When I eventually made it to the summit and was met by another DS, I was beyond elated. I knew I had finished the last big obstacle of the course. I was back on top of the Fan and it was all downhill from there.

I set off at a jog towards the far side of Pen-y-Fan and began my descent. I could see several Loadstoners in front of me and I tried to catch them as a personal challenge, however they were keeping to a pace slightly faster than me and they slowly disappeared into the distance. It actually took me a long time to get back down and I felt like I was going on forever. When I was on the final downward section and I knew the finish was only a few hundred meters away, I went flat out and sprinted for it.

I came across the line to cheers and handshakes. I was totally exhausted but I felt fantastic for doing it, and when I found out I had made it just within the Loadstone tier 3 time I was amazed. I had a chance of getting a Loadstone medal if I did well in the Point to Point event.

I received my Fan Dance medal and my certificate, and stuck around to cheer the other participants across the line. The camaraderie yet again was just incredible, and the atmosphere was electric. Apart from a slight navigational misunderstanding where I climbed over Cribyn, the event was a brilliant experience and TSFE staff were excellent. Although we were all doing these events in potentially hazardous locations, I felt safe and well looked after at all times. The directing staffs' professionalism was first class.

I stuck around for a while and we shared tales of the day again before I headed back to Plymouth. Just like before when leaving the SF10, I felt elation, and I was filled with excitement. This time I also had a glimmer of hope. Maybe, just maybe, if I did well on Point to Point I could earn myself one of the coveted Loadstone medals. Only time would tell.

Chapter 16

Point to Point

I spent the next 4 weeks with my face buried in maps of the Brecon Beacons. The final Loadstone event, Point to Point, is a 17mile (28km), self-navigation march in the mountains. It begins at the Beacon's Reservoir, where you are given a grid reference that you have to navigate to with map and compass. When you have reached that location, you will be given another grid reference for you to get to. It carries on like this until you are instructed to stop. With this in mind and no set course, I studied the whole of the Brecon Beacons area and made notes of all major peaks and features. I also continued to train at a high level and was still doing runs with a Bergan full of bricks.

Point to Point was held on the 4th July and the week leading up to it, I kept my eye on the weather in Wales, which was awful for that time of year. Constant heavy rain fell in the Brecon Beacons and I was dreading it doing the same on the day of the event. Navigation over mountainous terrain can be difficult at the best of times. It becomes a lot harder in poor visibility.

I drove up the day before and was plagued by showers as soon as I crossed the Severn Bridge into Wales. I was starting to think that I had been cursed. Surely it must go against the law of averages the amount of times I have had shitty weather on the events I've done!

I slept in the Hotel Skoda again that night, however this time it was a lot warmer. The moist humid July heat brought out millions of midges that took to biting me through the night, which caused me to get little sleep. The following morning I made my way to the rendezvous point at the Beacons Reservoir. AB and the other Loadstoners were there, but RL was not this time. RL had a bit of an injury on the Fan Dance event so didn't turn up for this last outing. RL and I would meet again. I went on to do specialist security and counter terrorism courses with him in Hereford, however that is another story entirely.

We Loadstoners got together as before and shared a laugh about what lay ahead. We had been whittled down from 30 plus to a mere 15 or so. I think it's important to state that one of us left in the running was a woman. Her name was CA, and to be honest she settles the argument of whether women have what it takes to be allowed into the Special Forces. Her endurance and resilience was exceptional, and she stayed shoulder to shoulder with the best of us during every event. She got treated the same as all of us men by the DS, and she had to carry the same weight as us in her Bergan too. Yet, she was still in the running after 15 other potential Loadstoners had fallen at the wayside.

There was a TV crew present again and a well-known ex member of 22 SAS. After the 3 soldiers had lost their lives on selection, the media began to ask questions about Special Forces training techniques and if the selection process was too brutal. I personally think it was a silly question to ask. Being in the military in general requires a high standard of fitness and discipline. As for the Special Forces, that is on a different level entirely. SAS soldiers go on operations miles behind enemy lines for months on end, they do high altitude drops at night, and travel hundreds of miles carrying unimaginable loads, and then they have to perform under pressure in battle conditions. That is why they have one of the hardest selection courses in the world. Lessons would be learned from the deaths of the three soldiers who died, however changing the selection process would be a foolish thing to do.

The DS ensured we had the minimum emergency equipment and weight needed for the march. Then the event director JB gave us all a briefing. He stated that he would send us off in pairs, or in threes, as it was safer to start that way and we could work together on navigation in the early stages. We all wished each other luck and got into small groups. I paired up with AB and another lad, and waited to be called forward. Several others started before us and this gave me time to fill up on food, and check my gear again.

When we were finally called forward, I felt my adrenaline surge. This was it. The last event. And one I just wanted to get stuck into. The DS read off the first grid reference we were to navigate to, and I knew where it was instantly. It was the far side of what is known in the SAS as VW valley, the VW standing for Voluntary Withdrawal. It is where a large number of potential Special Forces recruits quit as they finally break from the effort.

The three of us crossed the A470 then climbed over a small fence and entered the field behind. We then followed a thin muddy path that led at an angle up to the top of the hill. When we went over the ridge of the hill and began to descend into the valley beyond, I started to take in the sheer scale of it. It was immensely wide with an extremely steep slope down to a stream at the bottom, and on the far side was a vertical face of reeds and grass. The recent rain had made it a semi swamp too and the ground was a mixture of mud and sludge. Clouds obscured the top of the opposite side of the valley. Only when we started to go down did they clear slightly and I noticed a very small dot at the top with a TSFE flag next to it – our first checkpoint.

Descending was very treacherous and I found myself on my arse a few times before I reached the bottom. AB and I caught up with a few other Loadstoners here and we all started the climb together. Now, I have described many large hills and ascents in the previous chapters, but this one for me is the hardest thing I have ever had to climb even to this day. After a hundred meters I was on my hands and knees crawling and clawing my way up it. It was insanely steep and it just went on forever! There was a point when I got close to the checkpoint that I honestly thought I was going to pass out. My head was spinning and I couldn't catch my breath. When I finally made it to the DS, who was sat in a chair smiling and drinking a warm cup of tea, I was a broken man. I fell over on my side and just lay there. The DS piped up cheerfully "You can see why they call it the VW Valley now can't you?" He then went on "On SAS Endurance, the recruits encounter this at the 30 mile point." If I was this wreaked climbing it while still fresh, I couldn't comprehend doing it with 30 miles under my belt. I could see why so many quit here.

I sat there for a while and watched the others climb to join me. They all looked just as exhausted as I felt. When everybody got their breath the DS gave us the grid reference for the next checkpoint. There were 6 of us and we all set off together. This next section was largely flat but it was through long grass and there were many boggy sections. It was also misty at this level and we had to keep a constant eye on the compass so we didn't lose our bearing.

The next part is a bit sketchy in my mind, as I went from the next checkpoint to the one after our small group broke up. We all went at different paces and some of us just wanted to do the challenge alone. I have to admit I did make a slight navigational error along the way. I looked across to an adjacent hill and saw three orange Bergan covers crossing it. Thinking that three Loadstoners couldn't all be navigating in the wrong direction, I stopped and double checked my location. Indeed it was I who was heading in the wrong direction and I corrected myself immediately.

At the following checkpoint I met up with several other Loadstoners again and we set off together. This section was hellish. There were two ways we could have travelled to the following checkpoint, one way was through a very dense strip of woodland, and the other was across a section of marsh. We chose the marsh. It started off slightly boggy and got progressively worse, until it was literally knee deep in places. One lad who I got on very well with called RW, compared it to the swamps in old Vietnam War films. The female participant CA was in our small group through this marsh section and she fared better than the rest of us. While most of us were stumbling over in the mud, she glided across the clumps of grass that were dotted around. When I tried to do the same I would just slide off and get stuck in the sludgy mud.

Needless to say it felt like heaven when we finally made it out of the swamps. We were then on a tarmacked road that lead to the next checkpoint. I remember one of the lads behind me saying how he hoped they had a crate of ice cold beer there. It did make me laugh. The clouds had cleared away now and the sun came out in all its glory. I was glad of this at first, but as time went on it started to cause problems. I was getting though my water at a very rapid rate.

I'd started off with 2 litres of water in a camelbak (water bladder) I had stored in the top of my Bergan, and I had a half a litre bottle in my main pack that I would only use in an extreme emergency.

I was down to about half a litre of water in my camelbak when I got to the next checkpoint. The DS here fired very serious questions at us to ensure we were switched on and not in trouble. He asked if we had enough water and a source of food. I knew my water supply was depleting rapidly and I did not know just how many more checkpoints there would be or how much further I would have to go. Not wanting to show the DS I had doubts about having enough water I lied and said I had plenty. Knowing how many streams were in the area, I would have been happy to use one of my sterilisation tablets I carried in my supplies to purify water from it.

I understand the dangers of lying your way through checkpoints, and I wondered at the time if the three that had died on selection did the same.

When the DS was satisfied that I was safe to continue, he read off the grid reference to the next checkpoint. I didn't even have to look at the map to know where it was, I knew the numbers off by heart. It was the grid reference for the summit of Pen-y-Fan. I had to show the DS my current location on an ordinance survey map, the location of the next checkpoint (Pen-y-Fan), and what route I would take to get there. I picked a blade of grass so I could point clearly at the map and showed him my plan. My heart sank as I took in the compacted contour lines along my route.

When he finally sent me on my way I remember thinking "I hope I make it through this and I don't end up being a victim of these mountains too."

The climb from that checkpoint was another savage one, and when I reached the top, I was met with a brutal wind which took my breath away. The route to Pen-y-Fan was across more marsh land and then down to my old nemesis, the Roman Road. I met and passed a couple of other Loadstoners on this section. I was very focused at this point. I knew I had to climb Jacob's Ladder again and I just wanted to get to it as soon as I could.

When I spotted the Roman Road I took a detour along a ridge beside it so I didn't have to go down it again. The memories of constantly tripping over on it while doing the Fan Dance were still fresh in my mind. Little did I know that I would see the Roman Road again the following year.

I skirted Cribyn which I swear had more boulders on it this time than when I did the Fan Dance 4 weeks previously. Then I was confronted with Jacob's Ladder and the climb up the Fan. I started this climb next to another Loadstoner – RW. We chatted at first until the slope got too steep and we lost our breath. We stayed together however and quietly motivated each other. When I felt like stopping he'd encourage me, and when he slowed I'd wait for him. It was fantastic to go through this experience with someone else, and it made the climb so much easier than trying to get through it alone.

We were met by two DS at the top, who obviously enjoyed seeing the state of those who had just climbed the Ladder. They smiled broadly as they read off the next checkpoint. I located it on the map and saw that it was the Beacons Reservoir from where we started. I asked if that was our finish point. The DS were just blank faced and said "You'll have to see when you get there."

RW and I set off together. We knew the route down from the Fan well and how to get to the Reservoir by following the A470. Feeling that we were coming to the end of the event I felt fantastic. I was aching all over, my feet were in constant pain, I had blisters all over my shoulders from my Bergan, but I was elated that I had actually gotten this far. As we approached the Reservoir we could see a few Loadstoners already there, and we ran in together.

We were met with handshakes and congratulations from our fellow Loadstoners and the DS. It was another emotional experience I shall never forget. I went to my car, got changed quickly, made a brew and went back to the finish line to greet the others as they came in.

The atmosphere was brilliant and as more participants came in we all swapped tales from the day. Some had navigated in different directions and taken alternative routes, and one person had missed a checkpoint entirely. Quite how he had managed to do this, then find the other checkpoint afterwards without being given a grid reference is beyond me. Luck must have been on his side.

As we were talking someone asked "Who's that?"

We all looked up to where they were pointing. There was a huge hillside across the other side of the A470, which had a near vertical face. A small figure with orange on top of their pack was coming down the front of it. We all started laughing, we were saying just how crazy and dangerous it looked to be coming down something so insanely steep. When the figure reached the bottom and crossed the road, I saw it was AB. It was a fantastic way to end the event.

Shortly afterwards I was presented with my Point to Point medal by James Dunsby's dad, David. It was a great honour to receive my medal from him. I felt a profound sense of sadness as I shook his hand, for I had been given a medal for doing Point to Point, a march on which he had lost his son.

We were then gathered together for the Loadstone presentation. They read off the finishing times for the event and started calling names out. They announced the tier 1 and tier 2 Loadstone winners. Then they read off those who had earned a tier 3 medal. I was absolutely amazed to hear my name called out. I even had to ask the DS again if he meant me. I couldn't believe it. Not only did I complete the events, but I did it in a time that had gotten me "Badged" – a term given to those who pass Loadstone and receive the medal.

I had left the military many years previously but doing Loadstone brought back a feeling of camaraderie I hadn't felt in a very long time. I met a truly wonderful group of people and I have forged friendships with some that will last a lifetime. I

162

still regularly stay in touch with many Loadstoners, and RL and AB I have literally been messaging as I write this book.

Receiving my Loadstone medal from the event director.

TSFE run the Loadstone event twice a year now and simulate summer and winter Special Forces selection test marches. They have also ran "Continuation" courses that involve everything from parachuting to escape and evade. They are an incredible group of individuals and I highly recommend their events. It doesn't matter if you have a military background or not, TSFE will push you to your limits, and you will find out yourself just what you are capable of.

Chapter 17

In His Honour

After Loadstone, I found it very hard to go back to doing smaller runs again, such as half marathons. They just didn't have the appeal they used to, as they were no longer a challenge for me. Loadstone also gave me back a confidence I hadn't felt since being in the forces, a feeling of being able to get through any challenge I am confronted with, either physical or mental. There was simply no going back to doing small events again.

Within a few days of returning from Wales, I found myself online looking up more challenges, and I instantly stumbled on the Bear Grylls Survival Race being held in London on October 4th. The advert for it bragged that it was the ultimate multiple obstacle course race, with various "survival" challenges along the way. There were two categories. I could either do a single 10km lap of the course, or do three laps and go for the Ultimate Survivor medal. Fresh off the back of Loadstone, there was no way I was going for anything less than the Ultimate Survivor category.

Yet again, Claire supported me all the way and told me to go for it. This time, however, I did have to discuss if the life insurance covered me for doing these events, especially this Bear Grylls one, which had a waiver stating that should I die on the course due to anything from snake bites to being shot I wouldn't sue the race organisers. I jokingly told Claire that should the worst happen to me on any of these events she should transport my corpse back and pop me in the kitchen, then say I had some kind of mishap.

AB from Loadstone messaged me saying he was doing the Bear Grylls race too, however he was traveling to London the day before I was and he was doing the single lap option. Unfortunately I didn't get the chance to meet up with him.

So on October 4th I found myself yet again in a large crowd waiting for the off. I could describe this race in fine detail but that would take several chapters in itself. All I can say is the Bear Grylls race was the craziest event I have ever done so far. It started off nicely with scramble nets and commando walls, then it got more severe with a 30 foot rope climb and a river run. There were many, many more obstacles along the way that were all intended to destroy our upper body strength. There was a jerry can and ammunition box carry at one point, which gave me flashbacks to Loadstone, and also a Bergan load carrying section with all the weight at the bottom of the pack for added pain, and that was only lap one. At the end of each lap I was tasked with doing extra "survival" challenges, everything from shooting targets with an air rifle, to manual fire lighting. After lap two I was feeling the pain, and lap three was nothing short of fucking horrible. Almost all of us had lost the upper body power to do many of the obstacles, so we had to resort to doing push-ups as a punishment. There were a couple of places on the course where we had to leap over piles of logs that were on fire. On my last lap I tried to jump over one such obstacle and fell right in the middle of it. I leapt out and rolled over in the grass, fearing I could have set my clothes on fire. Luckily I hadn't, although I honestly do not know how I didn't get severely burnt.

By the time I crossed the finish line, I was absolutely caked in mud, and I had multiple cuts all over me. As I was due in work the following day, I had to get back to Plymouth that night, so I went straight from the finish line to the tube station. I had no hotel to get washed and changed in so I got on a train back to Plymouth still covered in mud and blood, and smelling of the fire I had fallen in. The train was packed, however I found myself having a double seat to myself as no one would sit next to me! Although it was very tough, I thoroughly enjoyed the Bear Grylls race and I still find myself now and then gazing upon my Ultimate Survivor medal and smiling.

I enjoyed the format of the Bear Grylls race so much I entered several other multiple obstacle races. Although they were not of a great distance; most being only 10k, the many obstacles such as net climbs and river crossings made an otherwise unchallenging distance a mini adventure.

One thing that I really wanted to do after I completed Loadstone was SAS Endurance, also known as Long Drag. It is a 40 mile load carry over the Brecon Beacons, and is the final march of SAS selection. A couple of ex Special Forces companies arranged for the event to happen, however they pulled the plug before it could be organised. Being it has a 24 hour cut off and the sheer size of the route covers almost all of the Brecon Beacons, it is a logistical nightmare for a civilian company to run such an event. With multiple participants potentially spread over such a huge area, and in differing states of physical and mental exhaustion, it would be too dangerous to run.

Not being able to do SAS Endurance, I put in an entry for another TSFE challenge – Fan Dance Gemini. It involved doing two back to back Fan Dance marches on two consecutive days. I did these on the 4th and 5th of June 2016, and I opted for the full load carrying category. It was fantastic doing another event with TSFE and I got to see several familiar faces: those I had done Loadstone with, and the DS too. This event was especially hard, not just physically but mentally. I hated the Roman Road from Loadstone, and travelling down it a total of four times in two days on Gemini was beyond the realms of torturous. There is a video of me climbing Jacob's Ladder on the second day of Gemini, I am hunched over shuffling forward under my Bergan, and all you can hear is me chanting Claire and our boys' names. When things get tough, my thoughts of them can get me through anything.

I took a break from endurance events after Gemini and concentrated on doing tactical military training up in Hereford. This was a direct result of people I had met through TSFE. I will not go into detail in this book about it, I will say however that it gave me a deep insight into the training techniques of 22 SAS, and we should all be glad that they are on our side because you really don't want to be going up against them.

In late April 2018 I received a phone call from my brother Sean saying that my dad had had a stroke. He never recovered from it, and 2 weeks later on 9th May he passed away. He was aged 83. Growing up, my dad scared the hell out of me, his booming broad Irish accent and gigantic size made him a formidable figure. His presence alone would silence a rowdy room. As an adult however, I drew massive strength from him, for he and my mum came from a time when people never knew what giving up was, be that in a confrontation, a relationship, or achieving a goal. Even though I moved away from Coventry many years earlier, his influence had still been enormous. My weekly phone calls to him (which I still dearly miss) gave me huge encouragement in the challenges I faced over the years. I would not be the person I am today if it were not for him. His raging internal fire radiated to me.

I travelled back up to Coventry for my dad's funeral. When I, along with my brothers, Kevin, Sean, and Stephen, carried my dad's coffin on our shoulders into the chapel, I felt an overwhelming sense of loss. My mum couldn't attend as she was now suffering from end stage dementia, and although she would go on to pass away in July of the following year, in my mind she died first, her body was here but her spirit had left long ago.

My dad and mum – Chris and Mary.

In the following weeks after my dad's funeral, my brother Sean and I arranged to go over to my dad's birth city of Galway in Ireland, to do the official city half marathon in his honour. The Galway race wasn't until October, and I hadn't ran any real distances other than basic training runs since Gemini, 2 years previously. I started looked around for an appropriate challenge again, something to focus on to get me back into training. Nothing shorter than marathon distance.

I found several races that appealed to me, three especially. The 34 mile Dartmoor Crossing, the 34 mile City to Sea Ultra Marathon, and a 10 mile Dartmoor Volcano race. The problem was they were all on consecutive weekends. I hadn't ran any distance over 10 miles in the previous couple of years, could I do two ultra distance races and an extremely hilly trail event so close together? I would soon find out. As always, I pushed sense and reason to one side and just put in my entries for the races. It was 3 months until the Dartmoor Crossing which gave me plenty of time to train.

Many running books live by the religion that you have to do a very specific and set training program to build up to certain distances. This is not true. Of course, injuries are almost guaranteed if you just go out untrained and start running like crazy, but if you push yourself to new limits each run, even if they are small, you will experience large gains in fitness and distance in a very short period of time.

With a few weeks of being back into training properly, I could run 20 miles quite easily. The Dartmoor Crossing soon came around and I was excited about doing an ultra-distance trail event again. The Dartmoor Crossing starts in Belstone on North Dartmoor, the route then traverses the moor via Princetown, and finishes in South Brent on the southern part of the moor. This event was fantastic, I relished being back out there in nature, miles from anywhere and just enjoying the scenery. I ran past many places where I had done training exercises in the forces, and it brought back fond memories. It also highlighted the sheer barrenness of Dartmoor. There were a few times when there was nothing in any direction, not even a tree for as far as my eyes could see. It was just a sea of knee high grass blowing in the wind.

It felt brilliant finishing the race and I looked forward to the City to Sea the following weekend. I recovered quite quickly after the Dartmoor Crossing. Within 3 days, my aches started to fade and I was confident that I could do another 34 miles without too much trouble.

City to Sea ultra marathon starts in Exeter and takes a coastal route past Teignmouth, it then gets very hilly towards the end of the race which is in Babbacombe. Claire and our boys came to cheer me on this time and it was fantastic to have their support. The first 15 or so miles were largely flat and a dream to run. When it did start to get hilly though it was brutal. The views were spectacular and the coastline along this stretch of Devon is just beautiful, but the climbs over the headlands were absolutely draining. The biggest climb of all was right at the very end of the race, where I had to ascend a set of steps from Babbacombe Beach to the top of the cliffs some 70 plus meters above. There is a monorail that is next to the steps, and people were on it, mouths gaping as they stared at us runners going up the steps.

I reached the top a wobbling mess yet again, and staggered towards the finish line where I was greeted by Claire and the children. It was another brilliant experience. City to Sea and the Dartmoor Crossing are races I will definitely do again. They truly are trails with tales.

It took me longer to recover from the onslaught of the City to Sea hills than the Dartmoor Crossing. I was still aching the day before the Volcano race some 7 days later. Although only 10.5 miles, the Volcano race has over 550 meters of ascent and traverses some notoriously boggy areas of the southern moors. It starts and finishes in the village of Scoriton, and takes a circular route over the moors, including South Dartmoor's highest point – Ryders Hill.

This event, although brutal, was another crazy race. I ran through bogs that day that I thought I would never escape from. My whole memory of the event is just a blur of mud and madness. It was pure insanity, but great fun, and I would definitely recommend it to anyone who wants to see just what Dartmoor has to offer.

I had proved to myself yet again that I could take a break from doing long distance and adventure races and get back into them quite easily. Doing 3 races in 3 weekends after a 2 year break hadn't actually been that difficult. It was almost October now, and time to bid a final farewell to my dad in Ireland.

My brother Sean and I flew from Birmingham to Dublin, then travelled up to Galway by bus. I wished my dad could have been there to tell me the tales from his childhood, and explain his reasons for leaving Ireland, these were things he rarely talked about to us growing up. We did locate the house he lived in as a child though. It had now been converted into a shop that sold woollen clothes.

I fell in love with Galway City instantly, I marvelled at its many quaint little streets all bustling with life and filled with music and merriment. The ever present force of the North

Atlantic was always there though, blasting ice cold winds and sea spray along the shoreline.

We were blessed with sunshine on the day of the half marathon, which came out just at race start, and my brother Sean said "There's dad coming out to wish us luck."

I ran that race like no other. There was no physical hardship, no mental struggle to carry on. I just thought of my dad and my own little family all the way around the route. I had everyone I ever cared for and loved in my heart and head every step of the way around, and I ran that race for them.

After the incredible feeling of loss I felt when my dad passed away, I began to feel a profound feeling of warmth and admiration, a feeling of honour that I had this great man as my father. If there is one important thing my dad's loss has taught me, it's this – we never truly die. If we influence others, be that through parenting, teaching, friendship or love, we live on through those we have touched. For my dad will be with me in spirit every time I play with my wife and children on the beach, every time I encounter new challenges, from every sunrise to every sunset, until my own last breath. For my own lovely little family ride on the shoulders of this mighty giant's legacy.

I crossed the finishing line that day, floating on a cushion of air.

My brother Sean went back the following year and did the Galway half marathon again. This time he went with one of my other brothers, Stephen. I was due to go too, but unfortunately my personal circumstances changed and couldn't make it, as my eldest son Logan was diagnosed with Type 1 diabetes.

My brother Sean and I after the Galway half marathon.

Chapter 18

An Uninvited Guest

With Claire and I both having medical back grounds, her being a veterinary nurse for 30 years and me being an ex-combat medic, we tend to be very switched on regarding signs and symptoms in people and animals. So when our eldest son Logan, who was 9 years old at this point, started going to the toilet multiple times at night and drinking excessively, we knew there was something wrong. He was also losing weight rapidly, which is a red flag especially in children who should be growing.

We had a sample of Logan's urine tested and it showed he had extremely high glucose levels, and ketones were present. If your cells do not get enough glucose, your body burns fat for energy instead. This produces a substance called ketones, which can show up in your blood or urine. Ketones can turn your blood acidic, and when they show in urine, they are a major sign of type 1 diabetes.

Logan's diagnosis was devastating for all of us as a family. Learning that your son will have to inject insulin for the rest of his life or die is heart breaking. The moment Logan was told by a doctor that he had type 1, it destroyed him. He broke down in fits of tears and, although Claire and I were there to support him, he must have felt so very alone. I would give my life to take this burden off him, however it was something we had to come to terms with, and Logan did that amazingly.

Our journey as a family through Logan's diagnosis is documented in my book – Type 1 Diabetes: The highs and lows of diagnosis. I wrote it to help other families who are coming to terms with this life-changing disease.

The information booklet we were given at the hospital described type 1 diabetes as an uninvited guest within your home. That is very true, we never wanted this in our family, and there was nothing we could have done to avoid it. We would just have to learn to live with it and control it.

Logan who, was reluctant to have injections at first, progressed to doing his own blood sugar tests within a week of being diagnosed, and injecting himself shortly afterwards. His ability to come to terms with type 1 was, and continues to be, inspirational. Type 1 diabetes affects the whole family and Logan's younger brother Owen has been a pillar of support to him too. When Logan first started injecting, Owen would go up and hug him afterwards. I was so proud of both of them.

Proving that diabetes was not going to hold us, or more importantly Logan back, I entered him and his brother Owen in a race. I was down for doing a 24 hour endurance race called the Hope 24 near our home in Plymouth. My event involved doing as many 5 mile laps on a trail course within a 24 hour period. There was a children's category, a 2.4 mile course run before the main event. So I put the boys in for that.

The day of Hope 24, 2019 was truly amazing. It was a bright sunny June day and the sky was crystal clear. The race start and finish is in a very large field close to Dartmoor, and it was rammed full of tents. It resembled a large music festival, minus the bands. There were countless stands selling everything from running equipment to beer, and everybody was in high spirits; it was fantastic. I have never been to a running event with such a tremendous atmosphere.

Claire and I joined the boys on their 2.4 mile race. There were many other children and parents going around too. It was brilliant to see so many children running and enjoying themselves out in the wilderness and not stuck indoors.

Owen and Logan were off like rockets, and Claire and I had to physically hold them back and get them to slow down. 2.4 miles isn't far in the grand scheme of things, but Owen was not much taller than my waist and had little legs, so I was afraid he would tire early on going at such a pace. They both proved me wrong though. Logan and Owen ran every single step of the way without faltering. We all came across the finish line as a family, and it was a truly wonderful experience.

After many hugs and congratulations, I bid Claire and the boys farewell and they headed home. I went to my car, which was now an updated version of my old Hotel Skoda. The original Hotel Skoda I had to scrap out as I eventually ran it to death doing a close protection and body guarding course up in Hereford – it's a long story! I then prepared myself for the race, which I actually hadn't trained for.

Me, Logan, Owen, and Claire, finishing the hope 2.4 as a family.

In the months leading up to Hope 24, I had been focused on Logan and his diagnosis. My training had largely gone out of the window. I still ran regularly, however the distances were very small. Entering this race, I only expected to do 3 or 4 laps (15 to 20 miles), after all you get the same medal if you do 5 miles or 100 miles so it didn't matter.

Much like every other race, it starts off crowded and you all get into your pace and spread out. This course is quite wide and I let the whole field pass me just so I could enjoy myself and not be banged around. Right from the start I loved it. The large country estate we were on is a mixture of woodland, grassy hills and trails. It had everything I loved about trail running and I was in my element. Although untrained for this event, I knew after lap 1 that I was going to do more than I anticipated earlier.

I spent the day just plodding around at a slow pace and enjoying the moment. I didn't pay attention to how far I had gone, or even how much my legs hurt. I just kept thinking about everything I had achieved up to that point. No, I wasn't a millionaire, I don't own a luxurious car, I don't even own my home, but I have something more important that money cannot buy – my little family.

I once heard someone say "If you want to feel rich, then count the things you have that cannot be bought with money." I counted 3 – Claire, Logan and Owen. I couldn't be richer.

I ran on until the sun set and then went to my car. I had covered 40 miles without even thinking about it. I took a break, chatted with other runners and even sat down and had a few beers. I had a quick sleep and woke up at 2am. It was raining hard on the roof of my car and the wind had picked up. It didn't deter me though, I thought "I'm still in a race, I think I'll go out and do another lap."

I re-joined the race at 2:30am in the pouring rain. My bellowing breath was illuminated by my head torch as I took off into the night. I don't think I've ever felt so alive. The trails were muddy torrents, the fields were now like swamps, and the rain ran down my back, but I felt amazing. I would encounter other runners, their blazing head torches cutting through the rain and darkness, and they were all full of cheer, laughing and joking. This was what living was all about, not warm Jacuzzis and being pampered. It was about feeling every moment. I went on to do another 20 miles before the cut off time, and I enjoyed every one of them.

On events like Hope 24, I see the best of us as humans, I encounter runners of all races, religions and backgrounds. It doesn't matter what size a person is, what language they speak, or how much money they have, we are all going through the same harsh experience and finding the best in ourselves.

6 months after Hope 24, however, we would all see the worst of humans too. Coronavirus, which was at first just a small item on the news in a faraway land, fast progressed to knocking on all of our doors. In a very short period of time, we had all gone from doing as we pleased and being free to fly literally anywhere in the world, to being confined to our homes. At first, people showed amazing resilience and compassion for each other, then panic buying ensued and many showed their true selfishness.

For people like me that participated in running events, it was a terrible blow. I was training for another 100 mile attempt, a 117 mile event called the Devon Coast to Coast. This, along with every other event, were cancelled or put on hold, but this void in actual events was swiftly filled with virtual events, where you could do set distances of famous running routes without having to travel far from your home. There was instantly hundreds of medals up for grabs for those who were stuck at home and couldn't enter "real" races.

I was reluctant to do these virtual events at first as I saw them as cheating. I asked myself "How can I hold a medal that says I have done the Isle of Man ultra marathon, when I have only ran that distance around my own city?"

After several weeks of lockdown though, I was going stir crazy being stuck in and I needed a challenge again, so I found an appropriate virtual one to go for. It was the Climb Everest challenge. To earn the medal for it, I had to accumulate the height of Mount Everest from sea level (29,029 feet) on a GPS device and send in my daily results to an administrator to prove what I had done. There is a hill just down the road from my house that I opted to use, it is just over 200 feet in height. So I took to running up it to build up to the required height. Like all training, it was hard at first. The first 2 days I did it, I only managed it to the top 8 times the first day, and 10 the second. However I persevered and within a week, I was going up and down 20 times in one session. On the final day, I managed to do 27 ascents and descents. Dog walkers and locals looked on at me like I was crazy, and when I told them what I was doing it for, they confirmed to me that I was. By the time I finished the challenge, I had ran up and down that hill 146 times. Yes it was hard work, but it took my mind off the lockdown.

It is September 2021 as I write this, and although lockdown is over and things are returning to normal, Coronavirus is still causing restrictions. Only recently have I started to get back up to the level of training I was doing before it struck.

I have still yet to achieve my goal of running 100 miles, but I know I will, and when I do, I'll want to do it again to prove to myself it wasn't a fluke the first time around. Although I am writing this book, documenting my running experiences, these are still early days for me, for I am only 47 years of age. I follow many inspiring ultra runners who are still doing 100 miles races well into their 60s and even 70s. We all age differently and I may not be that lucky, but if I can't run, then I'll take up cycling instead, and if that fails I'll do wheelchair racing. Ever since I first started running as a child to avoid school bullies, I have always wanted to know just how far I can go.

Chapter 19

Fear

Here we are at the end of my running tales. I have included many of the races that I have participated in over the years, but not all of them, as there are far too many to include in a single book. As I have stated in the previous chapter there will be many more races to come. I do wish to say a few words before I go over the finish line of this book. It's about the one thing that affects all of us – FEAR. Fear is a crusher of dreams, it stops people more than anything else from achieving their true potential. I'm a member of a lot of running pages on Facebook and even a co-administrator of one. So very many people doubt their own abilities on these pages, and many say things such as "I cannot ever see me running a 5k/10k/half marathon", or "My body isn't designed for running!" Total rubbish!!!

We are all designed for running, huge distances in fact. It was only a few thousand years ago we were hunting for food and traveling great distances on foot every day in search of our next meal. Running long distances and achieving physical goals is mostly in the mind. Us humans now rely upon cars as a mode of transport, and this has caused many to frown upon using physical effort as a means to get around, because they fear the aches and pains that my come from doing such a thing.

When I first started running around my school track in my late teens, I couldn't make half a mile before having to stop. Since then I have ran countless half marathons, I've done 20+ ultra marathons ranging in distance from 32 to 71 miles, and I have carried a heavy Bergen over the Brecon Beacons many times in horrific conditions. However I pulled through and made it. I am nothing special, every single one of us can achieve these things, and a lot more too. The one thing that stops people is fear.

It is soul destroying, seeing so many people feeling helpless due to fear, be that a fear of failure, pain, or physical and mental abuse due to bullies.

This is what I've learned over the years - No one is afraid of heights, they are afraid of the fall. No one is afraid to play, they are afraid to lose, and no one is afraid of the dark, they are afraid of what may be hiding in it. Fear is in the mind, not the body. Those who fear something instantly give it power over them. The things you fear are undefeatable, not by their nature, but by your approach. Courage is not the absence of fear, but rather the judgement that something else is more important than fear. The brave one is not the one who has no fear, but the one who fights even though he is scared.

I used to be bullied badly as a child in Coventry, but now I will not let anybody, no matter who they are, intimidate me in any way, because I have no fear of losing a physical or mental fight. I would rather swallow blood than pride. Also, you can discover what your enemy fears most by observing the means they use to frighten you. Fear can cause small things to cast big shadows, but what you need to do is cast an even bigger shadow over it. Remember, no one controls you but you.

Fear kills more hopes and dreams than what the passage of time or growing old has. Fear is a terrible reason not to do something, just because a mountain is big doesn't mean you shouldn't try to climb it. If you make it to the top, fantastic, and if you don't, at least you tried and you'll have a story to tell for attempting it. I strongly believe that no one ever truly fails a task, they simply learn how not to do it. Every failure is a valuable lesson, it teaches you that you should take a different route or approach the next time you try, but it shouldn't stop you from trying again.

I understand that there could be some people reading this with disabilities that may be incapable of running, or even walking. If that is the case, then try to find another goal in life, maybe a hobby such as model building, fishing, or even writing. Every person on this planet has at least one story to tell, and some stories simply ache to be told.

It is important to have a passion in life, be it your family, hobbies, or even your pets.

Also try to have no heroes. Sure, admire people you are passionate about and take inspiration from them, but look up to no one, for if you do, the best you'll ever be is second. Don't try to be the next Arnold Schwarzenegger, or Sylvester Stallone, be the first YOU! Walk tall and cast a long shadow, do not stand in the shade of someone else's.

I wish you all the best of luck with whatever you try to achieve in this life, make every day count and always go for your dreams, otherwise they will remain just that – dreams.

Acknowledgments

First I would like to thank my amazing wife Claire, who has supported and encouraged me in every single thing I have gone for. When I have doubted myself and felt like giving up, she has kicked my behind and gotten me motivated again. Without her I would not have finished, or even entered, many of the races mentioned in this book. She truly is my soulmate.

I also wish to thank my eldest son, Logan, for giving me boundless inspiration. His ability to live with type 1 diabetes yet still push himself to the limits is incredible. I also wish to thank him for being my editor. Even at 11 years of age, his grammar and spelling are far superior to mine, and although I'm sure there are still mistakes within these pages, there would be a lot more without his input.

I can never thank my wonderful son Owen enough for all the happiness and joy he brings into our lives. His energy and sense of humour can fill the darkest of days with brilliance. This world would not be the same without him. He is my sunshine.

I would also like to thank those who have trained me in the Regular and the Territorial Army over the years. We may have had a few fall outs from time to time, but every incident made me a stronger person.

I have also trained and ran with many people over the years, far too many to list here. They all know who they are and I wish to thank you all for being there by my side.

Also a huge thank you goes out to all the race organisers, and those who volunteer their time so that people like me can do these crazy and amazing races.

I will end by thanking the family I came into this world with, my brothers – Kevin, Sean, and Stephen, and my mum and dad – Mary and Chris. It wasn't easy growing up where we did in Coventry, however I would not be the person I am today if I didn't. We never had much money and it was very tough at times, but I always felt loved, and that alone is the best present a child could ever have.

Printed in Great Britain
by Amazon